HARNESSING ANGER

HARNESSING ANGER

The *Way* of an American Fencer

Peter Westbrook

WITH TEJ HAZARIKA

SEVEN STORIES PRESS / New York

A Seven Stories Press First Edition.

Published by Seven Stories Press
632 Broadway, 7th Floor
New York, NY 10012

In Canada: Hushion House Publishing Limited, 36 Northline Road,
Toronto Ontario M4B 3E2

In U.K.: Turnaround Limited, Unit 3, Olympia Trading Estate, Coburg
Road, Wood Green, London N22 6TZ

10 9 8 7 6 5 4 3 2 1

Library of Congress Cataloguing-in-Publication Data:
Westbrook, Peter.
Harnessing Anger: The Way of an American Fencer/Peter Westbrook
with Tej Hazarika.
        p.   cm.
ISBN: 1-888363-39-8
1. Westbrook, Peter. 2. Fencing—United States—Biography. 3. Afro-
American athletes—Biography. 4. Afro-Americans—Ethnic Identity. 5.
Japanese Americans—Biography. 6. Japanese Americans—Ethnic Iden-
tity. 7. Fencing—Training—United States. I. Hazarika, Tej. II. Title.
III.Title: Harnessing Anger.

GV1144.2.W48W48 1996
    796.8'6'092
QB196-20258
    LCCN: 96-83817

Book design by Cindy LaBreacht

Printed in the U.S.A.

ACKNOWLEDGMENTS

I would like to give thanks: To my Master, for giving me all that I can possibly desire and more; to my dearest mother, who has crossed over to the other side, for teaching me to be disciplined and to love God; and to my wife, Susann, for being patient with me for so many years. To my sister, Vivian, who loved our mother so much, I pray that Mom's death makes her stronger. To my mentor, Csaba Elthes, who has crossed over to the other side, I send a smile. I also give thanks to my brothers in spirit, Mike, Bob, Herb, Gerry, and Don for the inspiration that keeps me going; to Tom Shepard, for initiating the creation of the Peter Westbrook Foundation; to the United States Olympic Committee, for supporting our youth; and to Alpha Alexander, for being a crusader. Finally, I wish to thank everyone who supports the struggle to enrich the lives of our youth.

CONTENTS

FENCING IS NOTHING
BUT CONCENTRATED LIFE.

—CSABA ELTHES

PART ONE

ON-GUARD IN THE GHETTO

1

All fencing action begins from the on-guard position. In sabre, the rear arm is brought down with the fist on the rear hip, to keep it out of the way of possible cuts. The sabre is held slightly low, with the point directed at the opponent's eyes. —*Sports Illustrated Book of Fencing*

My mother wanted me to fence. I thought she was out of her mind.

"I give you five dollar if you go try," she offered in her broken English.

"Why *fencing*, Ma?" I asked. I didn't know anyone who fenced, and hardly even knew what fencing was. I had no idea what to expect. Still, five dollars in those days was more like having fifteen dollars in your pocket today, and my mother was offering me five dollars for every lesson I took! I quickly dropped all my resistance to that strange white sport and started fencing lessons immediately.

It was 1967, and I had just entered high school in Newark, New Jersey. It was a turbulent time in America. The streets of Newark were blazing. In my neighborhood people were smoking reefer, popping pills, and getting in and out of trouble with the law. I saw men, women, teenagers, and cops fighting. I'd seen people killed on the street. Knives, bottles, hatchets, and billy clubs were more familiar to me than kitchen appliances. Just to get into my house every afternoon felt like a battle. Competition was something I had learned at an early age. But fighting was something different: a survival tactic that came to me out of necessity.

My mother wanted me to take up a sport that would draw my focus away from the streets and the violence of ghetto life. She knew that fencing would expose me to people from different backgrounds. That quick thinking on her part must have stemmed from memories of her own upbringing. Mariko-san Wada could trace her ancestry to samurai warriors in the service of the Japanese emperor. But who could have known that fencing would change my life completely?

My mother was no stranger to violence, even before her arrival in America. At the end of World War II, when the Americans bombed Japan, eighteen-year-old Mariko saw her mother blown up in the streets of Kobe.

It happened during a period of air raids, when the people of Kobe were running from location to location, trying to find the safest place for themselves and their possessions. Mariko and her mother were alone that day, moving their valuables from one place to another, when a bomb dropped nearby. After the explosion, Mariko found her mother's body lying face down in the street. Later, she saw her mother's corpse once again, heaped onto a pile of others in the back of a truck. These experiences left a deep emotional scar on Mariko that she would carry with her for the rest of her life.

After the nuclear bombing of Hiroshima and Nagasaki, Japan began a long process of reconstruction under the virtual occupation of the Americans. There were many U. S. soldiers in Japan at the time, and Ulysses Jonathan Westbrook, my African-American father, was one of them. I don't know the details of how my mother met my father, since she revealed precious little about that period of her life, but I do know this: Twenty-two-year-old Mariko Wada met and fell in love with a handsome black American GI who was stationed in Kobe. I imagine they were instantly attracted to each other. "Yourazy," as my mother called him, was twenty at the time. He was Mariko's first love. I think that he must have represented another world to her—far away from the nightmare she had survived.

Mariko's father, Sataro Wada, would hear nothing of it. The war had snatched away his wife, a son, his house, and all his possessions, and now his daughter wanted to run away with a soldier from the army that was responsible for these crimes. It was unthinkable. And not only was this soldier an enemy, he was black too!

Japanese society, unlike our own, is generally very tradition-bound. The Japanese might dress and consume like Westerners, but when it comes to marriage, they stick exclusively to their own kind. Even people of European descent are not readily accepted. So if the war hadn't made Ulysses Westbrook an enemy, he still wouldn't have been embraced as a friend. For all of these reasons, Sataro Wada was dead set against the idea of his daughter marrying this man.

"If you do that, we will disown you," he warned.

Surely Mariko feared the consequences of her actions. Yet she was brave, naive, and love-struck enough to do the unthinkable: she disavowed her father and her culture. She must have imagined that a whole new life awaited her in the land of the free, filled with great freedom and domestic bliss. And Ulysses, who grew up poor in South Carolina with seven brothers and sisters, probably imagined that to live in America with a pretty Japanese wife would afford him some distinction and a different way of life than the one he knew. Perhaps deep inside he also believed that by "rescuing" Mariko, he could rescue himself from the shame he felt over the horrors he and his country had wrought upon Japan.

In 1950, Mariko and Ulysses were married without any fanfare by the court of law. My sister still has the marriage certificate and the many letters Sataro Wada sent his daughter throughout the years. Soon after, Ulysses received his discharge from the army. It was time to go home.

The young couple set sail for Seattle, Washington, and then continued on to St. Louis. On April 16, 1952, shortly after they settled down, I was born.

My mother's family had been very wealthy on both sides. They were part of the Catholic minority in a society where most people were either Buddhists or Shintoists. Her father worked for the Japanese government in the Ministry of Internal Affairs. Before the war, the family had a grand piano, ticking grandfather clocks, and parrots all over the house. Household chores were taken care of by domestic help. Mariko had no idea until she got to the U.S. that my father was from a very poor background. Not knowing what to expect and coming from a wealthy Japanese family, the world of ghetto poverty must have been a shattering disappointment.

Within a year after I was born, my parents moved from St. Louis to Newark, New Jersey because four of my father's siblings, including his youngest brother, Olin, had all settled there. My father worked as a bartender while my mother stayed home pregnant with my sister, Vivian, who was born eleven months after me.

We lived in the Hayes Homes Projects in central Newark. They were one of the new urban reservations for poor people, a trap of ignorance and isolation from opportunities. The projects in New Jersey are different from those in New York. In Manhattan, even if you live in the projects, you can still see successful people walking in the neighborhood. But in the projects of New Jersey, we were completely cut off from the rest of the world. Hayes was an enormous and crowded complex—twenty or so buildings all clumped together, each twelve stories high. Hayes was brand new when we moved in, but the place quickly degenerated. It grew more vicious with the years, wasting many people before they could even begin to tap their potential.

My parents got along badly but they stayed together for five years, probably because of us kids. Their arguing was always one-sided, with my father handing out all the abuse.

I think part of the problem was that he just wasn't able to deliver what my mother expected of him. By the time I was four, I knew that there was something very wrong. My sister would always cry when they fought. I don't remember crying. I could only watch in horror and feel unconditionally sympathetic toward my mother. Sometimes I would wake up in the morning and find my mother and sister huddled together, crying in a corner of the apartment. After so much abuse, my mother couldn't take it anymore. Finally, some friends in the projects advised her to go to the police.

The police came to our apartment and took my father down to the station house. My mother told us how relieved she was. She was happy that the cops understood that Ulysses was beating up on his poor Japanese woman. At the police station, Dad was blinded by huge flood lights shining in his face while the cops hit him with hoses and pummeled him with blows. When he came back home, he was very badly bruised and swollen. "Punches were landing all over my body," he painfully groaned.

Eventually things got even worse. Social workers would show up at the door urging Dad to contribute something toward the family. He never did. Unprepared to cope with family responsibilities and with an Asian wife who was used to having more, our father succumbed to denial and alcohol. His mental and emotional condition quickly deteriorated. His plight was not so different from that of countless males in our country at the bottom of the social ladder. It seems that he just gave up trying to meet my mother's expectations and fell prey to the worst influences that plague our society.

This unhappy situation ended abruptly when my parents separated permanently. At first, my father elected not to come around. But after a while, he would come around occasionally, though he never brought us anything. We didn't get any financial or emotional support from him. I'm not quite sure whether I ever learned to look up to my dad in those first five years. It was my mother who always took care of us; she never abandoned us. Our well-being was always foremost in her mind. When we went to the movies, for instance, everybody would be buying popcorn, but not us, since we were always broke. Instead, Mom would make us popcorn and sandwiches to bring along. Such little acts of love and consideration went a long way. Much later on, my parents got a legal separation, since as a devout Catholic my mother didn't believe in divorce.

Yet there *are* happy memories of those times. My sister and I used to play together. I remember us wrestling with my father. I remember me dressing up in my sister's outfits and my sister dressing up in mine. We'd put on a little song and dance show for our parents. There was laughter.

Even though we didn't have many things like a lot of people, we were basically happy. Some Christmases I just got one toy—a big water gun or a toy rifle. And my sister got one tiny little doll. Sometimes we didn't get anything at all. My mother, hailing from wealth as she did, must have wondered how we viewed our circumstances, so from time to time she would ask us, "Are we rich or are we poor?"

"We're rich!" we would always respond. When we were grown, she told us how our answer charmed and amused her.

The truth is, I felt that we *were* rich as children. I think we felt this way because my mother gave us a lot of love.

Still, life in the projects was difficult. My sister and I were the brunt of cruel and ignorant jokes. Kids would call us names like "chinky chinky chink." I used to get beaten up. I had to fight every day. If I came home crying, my mother would be angry and would smack me for getting into a fight. I quickly understood that the stronger people preyed upon the weak, and learned not to appear weak under any circumstance. Now I know that it's okay to be soft and gentle. But in that neighborhood, if you showed any tenderness or affection, people tended to abuse you tremendously. I always felt like an outsider, like an outcast, never being accepted. This made me angry. I had to learn to fight, and I constantly felt the need to make myself stronger.

The thinking process of most people living in the ghetto is a little warped. They are really not a part of mainstream society, even if they do watch plenty of television. You don't realize it while you're in it. You don't realize it unless you are able to step out of it. I don't think it's possible for people who have only lived in nice environments to understand how tough it is for a child to grow up in the ghetto. That brutal environment taught me how to deal with adversity. How to deal in strength.

When my father left, my mother had no job. She had a hard time with English and knew nothing about the welfare system. Most people in the projects are poor, but we were poorer than poor. When we had no food, neighbors would bring us cans of Campbell's soup. When we had holes in our shoes, my mother would cut out pieces of corrugated cardboard from a box and insert them as insoles. I would go to school with cardboard in my shoes. Still, Mom maintained a comfortable home and instilled us with strong values. And we were never ashamed to be poor because we knew we were striving to do our best.

Repeatedly, Mom told us that the home had to be the most comfortable place because children have to be happy there. Even though she was a strict disciplinarian who believed in corporal punishment (then again, didn't everyone thirty years ago?), she was lenient in other regards. On weekends she let us stay up as long as we wanted—till 3, 4, even 5 o'clock in the morning. But I can tell you right now that if my mother hadn't been strict the rest of the time, we'd never have been able to pull ourselves out of the projects. She raised us the way she did for a reason, and I think she was smart. Mom gave us what we needed—she did it all herself.

Looking at all the domestic violence today, it seems that many women don't have the self-confidence to leave their husbands. My sister has helped me to understand that Mom was quite intelligent and forward-thinking in the way she handled her relationship with my father. Even though the marriage was difficult, she gave it a few years—which she considered fair—to see if it could be straightened out. When she saw that it was only getting worse, instead of staying with her husband and being miserable and abused, she bailed out. That was a pretty tough move to make in those days, especially for a single mother living in a foreign country without any family or friends.

My mother had the strength to kick out this man who was abusive to her, and she struggled to raise us, seeking refuge in the Catholic church with a God who neither abandoned nor abused her. She established a rapport with two of the priests at our church, Father Stalb and Father Yeo. They gave her the emotional support and the confidence that she needed to survive. She went to them when she had problems. When our father started being abusive, they helped Mom find the strength in herself to kick his butt out and leave him for good. Father Yeo even loaned her money sometimes. She would always pay him back when she got back on her feet again.

Contrary to popular opinion, most people in the ghetto don't go to church often. Surrounded by a sea of indifference, my mother was an island of tremendous faith. She wanted to pass this along to us by giving us a Catholic education. But poor as we were, we couldn't possibly afford the tuition. She begged the people who ran the school at our church, St. Peter's, to accept me for free. They turned her down, but she persisted, offering to work for them in exchange for my tuition, and they finally gave in. In return, my mother cleaned the priest's rectory, served drinks at bingo games, and helped out in any way she could.

St. Peter's was a relatively poor Catholic school where they crammed two or three grades into one class. When I started there, the school was integrated, but predominantly white. We had white teachers, white nuns, and white schoolmates. But when black people started moving into the neighborhood and joining the church, the white people opened up their own St. Peter's in another diocese. At our school, African-American nuns and administrators replaced the departing white nuns and administrators. A year later, when my sister Vivian came in, the school was renamed Queen of Angels. Only a handful of white students remained.

Prior to this "white flight," the interesting thing I remember was that although the white teachers were kind and helpful towards us, on the whole, the atmosphere at school was filled with tension. There was tension between poor kids and middle-class kids, between black kids and white kids, and between parents and teachers. I'm not implying that it is bad to be in an integrated school, but once the whites left and all those kind black nuns and black and Latino students moved in, things became much more relaxed and harmonious.

School turned out to be an invaluable place for me. There was virtually no one in the community where I lived that I could look up to or want to emulate. Naturally, I wanted to be tough like some of the guys around the neighborhood because I noticed that people didn't bother them. Still, I didn't really look up to them as heroes. It didn't feel right to me. The closest anybody came to filling that role were the teachers at school. Even though they disciplined us with slapping, kicking, spanking, and the classic smack of the ruler, they were basically kind and caring. I was able to talk to them and be affectionate with them. This was exactly the kind of interaction I couldn't find outside in the community. To get that kind of interaction at school was precious. I remember this clearly.

Although I can't recall a single living hero I looked up to as a child, I loved watching Zorro on television. He was my hero. Zorro was a swashbuckling Latino Robin Hood who presided over Southern California when it was still part of Spain's vast New World empire. Zorro would leave his characteristic "Z" mark with the tip of his sword after making his surprise attack on the latest bad guys—usually corrupt politicians. He was a people's hero, and they always protected him from the law. I actually thought, "I want to be like that!" I was such a fanatic about Zorro that every Halloween, I would ask my mother to buy me a Zorro costume. The image of the victorious Zorro on his beautiful horse, and the music from the show's theme song, "*Zorro, Zorro, Zorro!*" often stirred in my mind.

My mother raised my sister and me like soldiers in an army. At home, she would discipline us in her characteristically militaristic style. She was always yelling, "No, don't do that!" or "This is the only way!" or "Get up when I tell you to get up! When the clock rings, you stand up immediately. Up! Move! Out of the house!" She'd insist that we do our homework, but she rarely said, "Let me see your homework when you're finished." She trusted us to do what was asked of us.

In spite of her affluent background, I don't think my mother really understood what made people well-rounded. She wasn't enthusiastic about exposure to art or music, and she didn't seem to realize that performing in front of an audience can help children tremendously in building self-confidence. Of course, I have to remind myself that Mariko Westbrook was too poor to afford sending us to any special programs beyond school. But she firmly believed that the only thing you needed to succeed in life was hard discipline and good manners. She also believed that it was not the color of your skin or what you looked like or the kind of job you had or how rich you were—it was only the condition of your heart that really mattered.

When Mom finally got a nine-to-five factory job assembling light bulbs at the General Electric plant across the street from where we lived, we were able to afford some of the things we never had before. Eva, the lady next door, looked after us in her apartment every afternoon. Then, when Mom came home from work around 6:00 p.m., she would cook us some dinner.

As far as we knew, Mom was the only Asian in our neighborhood. But everybody liked her. They called her a Japanese doll. Men liked my mother because she was very beautiful. People made sexual offers to her, she was always telling me, but because of her strong religious beliefs she would always say no. People would even offer her money. Men liked her, women liked her, everybody liked her. But the sad thing is that in her own mind, she didn't feel accepted. I think what happened to her was this: After traveling halfway across the world with a guy who brings you to a foreign country and then beats you and beats you, your world is turned upside down. The world is no longer your friend. Your whole perspective changes. You look at the world through tarnished glasses. Mom would look at the projects and see all the negativity and would no longer trust people. "No good rats," was what she called people who had wronged her, especially my father. She got hurt so much in the projects, and nobody was

there to defend her. All that hurt made her angry and mis-
trustful. We lived in the Hayes Homes Projects for twelve
long years.

As I grew up, I found it increasingly difficult to communicate with my mother. It was not until much later that I
understood that there was a very lonely person inside her. I
was not very sensitive about her cultural isolation. Back then,
Japanese people were not looked upon by Americans as smart
and businesslike. They were only frowned upon. Again and
again, Mom would say, "If it wasn't for the grace of God, I
would lose my mind here!" She told Vivian and me that most
Japanese people would not be able live under such circumstances. "Don't you know how lucky you are?" she would ask
us. "I could have goback to Japan and left you!" Every time
we were out of control, she'd remind us about her Japanese
girlfriend who had just gotten up and left her American husband and two children when her husband got abusive. She
said that we'd better appreciate what she did for us and bust
our butts to make her efforts worthwhile. She'd repeat these
things so often that it got on my nerves!

Now I realize how hard it must have been in those days
for a Japanese woman to raise two kids in the ghetto with no
support, no roots, and no familiarity with the social and cultural environment. For twenty years, the only contact Mom
had with her family in Japan was an occasional exchange of
letters. And although my father came from a large family of
six brothers and one sister, his youngest brother, Olin, was
the only one we had any real connection with. He and his
wife were the only ones who helped. They would come

around now and then after my parents broke up to take us kids out. Other than that, for the better part of our childhood, my mother was really on her own.

When I turned fourteen, the winds of fate brought my father and me together again for a few months, but the meeting only sharpened the pain that I felt over him. It was just before I started fencing. I had hardly seen or heard from him for nine years.

As much as I loved my mother, her overprotectiveness and her insistence on discipline was becoming unbearable to me. No matter the weather or season, we always had to be home before dark. I couldn't cry in front of her because she would get angry or hit me. Once, in my early teens, she looked out the window and saw seven guys beat me up. When I returned to the apartment, I found her crying. We were both crying. She didn't say anything, except, "You got in a fight? What happened? Is that what happened? Okay." End of conversation. Until then, if I came home crying or complaining about somebody bothering me, she wouldn't hear of it.

Mom was fanatical about the most ridiculous things. For instance, she forbade me to wear a little Humphrey Bogart felt fedora because she thought only gangsters in the neighborhood wore hats like that. That, I thought, was going too far. She really believed that a hat would make a gangster out of me! She insisted on picking out all the clothes I wore. And when my friends and I would play the game of pitching coins for change, my mother would come down and slap me in front of everybody—and I don't mean gently, I mean with all her might. Then she'd tell me to go upstairs. Small things like that made me feel that I could no longer bear to live that way.

Well, I'll just go and live with my father, I plotted. Forgetting all the abuses he had meted out to my mother and sister, I phoned him. He agreed to take me in. When I told my mother, all she said was, "Go." So I packed a bag of clothes and headed to Dad's apartment in East Orange, New Jersey, where he was living with a girlfriend named Wilette.

Much to my delight, my father welcomed me with open arms. I felt that relief was finally at hand. Now I could act like an adult and not have my every desire squashed. Living with my father was a big improvement indeed. He had a nice apartment in a small brick building with almost no kids around—very different from the projects. But Dad was still abusive. He would beat Wilette, who would then try to bring me into their arguments on her side.

Over the three-month period that I was with him, he told me several times, "Peter, one day I might have to move to Florida and you might have to leave your mother—you might have to come with me. How do you feel about that?"

I wasn't sure what he meant and didn't really deal with the issue. All I could say to him was, "Aw, you're not going anywhere, you're just saying that."

But a few days later he would say it again. "Peter, one day I might have to leave New Jersey. If I do, do you want to come with me?" I still didn't take his question seriously.

The following week, when I came home from school one day and opened the door, everything was gone, even the furniture. Just that morning, with Wilette by his side, my father had given me a hug as I was leaving the apartment, and now the apartment was empty. What could I do? Where could I go? I looked in all the closets—all empty except for the bag of clothes I had brought with me. Then I found a note that said, "Here's twenty dollars. I'll contact you later." That was it. I fell right down on the floor and started crying.

I was so determined not to go back to my mother that I discussed the matter with Wilette's sister Ann, who lived in Dad's building. She couldn't believe what had happened and must have felt sorry for me because she let me stay with her and her baby daughter for six months. Ann was a nurse by profession and she had a boyfriend who would come around once in a while. I tried to help out by baby-sitting for her daughter when I could.

Months later my father called me—he must have known I was staying at Ann's place. "How are you doing?" he asked. I couldn't believe that was all he had to say. I was a kid and I didn't know how to talk about my feelings and I was so hurt by his abandoning me. I told him I was doing fine. He asked me again if I wanted to go down to Florida to live with him. I remember feeling really let down because he didn't show any remorse for having left me the way he did. By then, my mother had started calling me persistently to say that since I was not yet eighteen, I had no right to live at that woman's house. So I told my father I wasn't interested and that I would soon be moving back in with Mom.

Looking back, I see that it was my great good fortune to have the kind of mother I did. She instilled so many essential values in my sister and me. She taught us that we should never give up in our endeavors. She would literally tell us to not cry, to work hard, to be ethical, and to fight to achieve our goals. And if we should survive the fight, she said, we should get up and fight some more.

I was also lucky to have a mother who knew that fencing would keep me off the streets. But fencing did more than just keep me out of trouble. She correctly concluded that I would meet people who would expose me to a different world than the one I was used to. It wouldn't have been the same if I had taken up boxing in school. Now I happen to think that boxing is a very lovely sport, even if it is a bit barbaric. That might sound paradoxical, but what I mean is that it attracts a certain type. Other types of people are attracted to karate or kung fu, and still others are attracted to football. Since fencing and kendo (samurai-style fencing with bamboo sticks instead of swords) are both popular in Japan, my mother knew from experience that the people who were attracted to these sports tended to be educated, disciplined, and refined. And those were the kinds of people she wanted me to know.

This is not just a story about how I found a sport that provided an outlet for my energy and literally saved my life. It is not only about winning recognition and respect. Nor is it only about how discipline and concentration learned in fencing will open doors in other facets of life. Rather, this is a story about one man coming to understand the preciousness of life.

WEAPON, MIND, AND MENTOR

Boxing and running were my two favorite sports as a kid. Where I grew up, the brutal game of boxing was a popular neighborhood pastime—seeing who could hit the hardest and block the fastest. The most popular form of attack was the open-hand to the head. I was used to taking that kind of blow and was very good at dishing it out, with or without gloves on. Then there was running, which usually meant running from a bully or racing: "So, you think you're faster than me? I'll race you to the end of the block!" All any poor boy could do in the ghetto was fight to keep from being beaten up or run to save his life.

By the time I was fifteen or sixteen, I started being more confident and began to fight back. Truth be told, I actually loved to fight because I loved to defeat my enemies although conversely, I hated to be defeated. The more my fighting skills developed, the stronger I became. People stopped bothering me. I thought I was a warrior! Had it not been for my mother's strict supervision, I probably would have gotten involved with gangs. I often think about the kids from my neighborhood, how they never had a chance. I would say that 90 percent are dead, 8 percent are in jail, and I have no idea what happened to the remaining 2 percent. Stinky, Buddy, Carter, and Horse are the nicknames of some of my buddies that didn't make it. Drugs or homicide took their lives; one was shot in the back for robbing a store, another, murdered by a rival.

Essex Catholic High School was a predominantly white, all-boys school in Northern Newark, two bus rides away from where we lived. Essex had a great athletic program. It was the training ground for many successful sports celebrities, like Olympians Mark Murro and Marty Liquori, and baseball player Rick Cerone. In addition to the usual programs like track, baseball, basketball, and football, the school had fencing, one of its stronger programs.

My first fencing teacher was an Italian-American medical doctor named Samuel D'ambola. He had started the fencing program at Essex High just for the hell of it. Dr. D'ambola was a kind man who put his heart into training children. He had just the right ingredients to help me discover my talent.

Dr. D'ambola started me out with the sabre instead of the foil, which is the weapon most people start out with. I was glad. While the foil is considered a basic, all-purpose sword that is easiest for beginners to handle, the sabre is a military sword that was favored by cavalry captains and pirates of the high seas. It is a distinctive-looking weapon with a slightly curved blade and a curved knuckle guard which extends from the hand guard to the base of the grip. The sabre evolved out of the cutlass, and is predominantly a cutting and slashing weapon, the kind Zorro used for his "Z," *shoup, shoup, shoup.* Well, I had certainly done plenty of slashing and swinging with sticks, rocks, and bottles, but with a sword in my hand, I suddenly felt like a real-life Zorro at last!

In sabre fencing, the target area is everything from the hips on up, including the arms and the head. It's a freer style, more like jazz or modern dance. With the foil, on the other hand, the target area is the torso, excluding the arms and the head. You can only score with the tip of the blade, only with the point. No cutting, no slashing, only poking. Foil fencing is very elegant, kind of like ballet, with less movement and much more control. There is also a weapon called an épée, which was originally a dueling sword. It is similar to a foil, only a bit heavier and stiffer, with a larger hand guard. In épée fencing, the target area is the whole body, from head to toe. The best fencers in the world specialize in only one weapon, and the sabre felt just right for me.

I quickly became attached to sabre fencing. Fencing satisfied my constant need to be quick with everything I did. Since I was already a fighter, fighting with a sword instead of with fists or sticks came naturally to me. I loved being able to prove myself in one-on-one combat, to see if I could physically, mentally, and emotionally destroy my opponent. I would try to demoralize him to see how much abuse he could take. Fencing was just like street boxing, only not as brutal. And here was a kind of fighting that my mother not only allowed, but actually encouraged.

Everyone in the fencing program at Essex had started one or two years prior to me, but within a few weeks of starting, I was beating 80 percent of the people, and very soon after, everybody. Dr. D'ambola was confident enough to tell me that I had the ability to be a top sabrist in no time. I couldn't help thinking to myself, *This is great!*

Naturally, not all of my teammates had the same opinion. I soon had jealousy and rivalry to contend with. Being the only black kid in the program didn't make things any easier for me. I knew the laws of the jungle, and understood that I was on their turf. So I tried my best to be a gentleman and to be humble and amicable about the situation. It took about a year for most of the kids to accept me. As for the others, I had my ways of dealing with them. If I saw that there was nothing I could do to make them accept me, I would try to destroy them emotionally, just as they had done to me. There was one guy, a real big guy, who constantly harassed me and accused me of cheating him. I finally gave it to him in front of everybody until he was crying like a big old six-foot three baby.

Dr. D'ambola's training program was rigorous, and certainly kept me off the streets. We trained every day after school from 3:00 to 6:00 p.m., and traveled to competitions up and down the East Coast. We had the number one fencing program in the state of New Jersey, and hadn't lost a match in years. We always had incredible talent at Essex, like Bruce Soriano, who went on to win several NCAA titles, and Bruce's younger brother, Greg. In fact, we were so notorious that when we walked into the room at a tournament, our opponents were clearly afraid of us. It was a great feeling to be part of such a powerful team.

Winning brought me a feeling of acceptance that I never had before. While I didn't yet have the skills or the savvy I would acquire over the years, my raw talent, tough determination, fighting spirit, and sheer barbarism was enough to keep me winning. During my four years at Essex, I remained one of the school's top fencers, and in my junior and senior years, I was captain of the team. Dr. D'ambola was the greatest. I am still in contact with him. Whenever he reads about my victories in the papers, he calls to congratulate me and to tell me how proud he is. I will forever be grateful to Dr. Samuel D'ambola for recognizing my talent and encouraging me.

Fencing wasn't the only good thing that happened to me during my high school years. My family finally managed to get out of the projects. In 1968, we moved into the top floor of my uncle Olin's nice, three-family house on Shepard Avenue in the suburbs of Newark. We were still in an all-black neighborhood, but everyone owned their own home, with grass in the back—all that. For the first time in my life, I had my own bedroom. I really respected Uncle Olin for letting us live there. In his own way, he was kind of like a parent, always looking out for us.

Moving into a real house in a decent neighborhood was a great opportunity—our first springboard to mainstream society. But it wasn't an easy change to make. When I talk about getting out of the projects, I'm not just talking about a bunch of buildings, I'm talking about a whole way of life.

You know how they say, "You can take the person out of the ghetto, but you can't take the ghetto out of the person?" Well, I guess that was the problem for me. After living in a ghetto environment for so long, I couldn't shake that mentality just by moving away. I didn't feel entirely comfortable in the suburbs; I didn't really like it at first even though I knew it was an important step. It all seemed so quiet and clean that it made me feel kind of cold and secluded and empty. These middle-class folks were more private, more guarded, not as friendly as our old neighbors. It was so different from Hayes, where hundreds of us were thrown together, forced into close contact by the small size of the neighborhood. At Hayes, everyone knew everyone else's business. Sometimes I'd go back to the projects just to hang out the way I used to.

When we were still living in the projects, Mom started seeing a man named Eugene King. Mom and Gene, or "Genie," as we called him, were definitely "an item." Though Genie never moved in with us and never showed any physical affection toward Vivian and me, he came to be considered part of our family. He would spend his evenings and weekends with us, but would always return to his own home at night. Genie helped us pay the rent at Uncle Olin's place, and although he still kept his own apartment (as my mother insisted), he spent a lot of time with us there. The thing about Genie, who was half-black and half-white, was that while he never abused my mother or us, he did have a problem with alcohol. But he cared enough and had enough good sense to hand over most of his money to Mom so he wouldn't spend it at the liquor store.

Like Uncle Olin, Genie was very helpful in showing us the world that existed outside the ghetto. He represented freedom for us. We'd all pile into his big green Buick, and head off for a day of fishing, swimming, or shopping at the mall. Sometimes we would take off and wind up as far away as Maine or New Hampshire or even Montreal. Mom and Gene stayed together for over twenty years, but eventually they split up for good. Years later Mom told us that even though our dad was abusive, he was a much better listener than Genie.

Fencing was already opening my eyes to worlds I never knew existed, just as Mom had planned. Even though I was the only black kid in the program at Essex, because I was good at fencing and because of who I was as a person, the other kids befriended me. Most of my schoolmates were Italian-Americans who came from middle- and upper-middle-class families, from towns like Montvale and Montclair. At first I felt uncomfortable around them socially and was scared to open up. I wondered, *What do these white kids think of me? Do they know how poor I am?* But over time I managed to relax, and I learned a lot by getting to know them. I found out how they thought, how they lived, what they ate, how they felt about black people, and how different their lives were from mine. I remember that when I told them about the good things my mother fixed for dinner—hog maws, collard greens, grits, neck bones, pig knuckles—they didn't even know what I was talking about!

I think it was also easier for them to accept me because of my Japanese side. They would tell me, "Pete, don't say you're black 'cause you're not. Your mother is Japanese."

They didn't want me to be black, plain and simple. By the same token, I used to tease my buddy, "Ah, Don Corleone," and he would get a little annoyed. In any event, for whatever reason, they seemed to look at me differently than they looked at other blacks. And when they invited me to their homes, I would always oblige, being very respectful and polite.

Some of these Italian families were really connected. At school functions when everybody was formally attired, one gentleman, the father of one my fencing buddies, would always come in dressed like a blue collar worker. Nevertheless, people like Tony Imperial, who was running for state senator, and Newark's Mayor Adonizio would walk up to this man's table and bow real low. Other people would kiss the back of his hand. I couldn't understand it at first, but then I realized that even though he only ran a tiny flower shop, he owned multiple cars and homes.

Many of these connected, community-minded dads would come around to visit my mother because of my fencing and because she was an active member of the Catholic community. One day the flower shop owner himself came to visit. He went upstairs to see Mom, and left his car in the middle of our street with the doors wide open. I remember how the other cars were honking wildly, trying to attract the absent driver's attention. A lot of these dads acted as if they owned the whole world. But regardless of our friendly relationships, we never called them for any favors.

By my senior year, I was the best fencer that Essex had. I was a B student and I liked math, but my only goal for the future was to be the best high school fencer in New Jersey. Nothing more. My mother was pushing me to go to college, but I wasn't really motivated to go because no one else in the neighborhood went. Children whose parents and neighbors are blue collar workers do not normally aspire to be doctors or journalists. They have no knowledge of the nature of such fields and the benefits that can result from training for such a profession. So, like most of my buddies, I had no idea what I wanted to be.

Somehow it never dawned on me that my fencing could lead to something bigger, that there were people out in the world who might look at me favorably. Then I got a recruitment call from New York University. Hugo Castello, the big coach at NYU, had his eye on me for his team.

Four years of high school fencing had earned me a full scholarship to New York University, complete with on-campus housing. You can imagine how happy this made my mother, but as for me, I had no idea what it all meant. What would I do there besides fence? What would I study? Would I finish the full four years?

At Essex, people around me were talking about college. Before I got the recruitment call I didn't pay them any mind, but now I had to find out what it was all about. "College?" I'd ask my schoolmates, "Why are you going to college? What do you do there?"

"Oh, Pete! You get an education and a degree!"

"Well, okay. If you guys are doing it, I might as well do it, too." So I decided to go along with the crowd. Somehow, it just seemed like the right thing to do, and I knew how much my mother wanted me to. At least I'd be fencing. As for the rest of it, I'd have to figure that out along the way.

Moving to Greenwich Village in 1970 was the biggest culture shock I ever had. The Village was rocking with revolution. The protest movement against the war in Vietnam was gathering nationwide momentum, and a day didn't pass without some kind of demonstration happening on campus and in the streets. Washington Square Park was the site of a nonstop celebration of Afros and laid-back longhairs smoking reefer and dancing to war drums. People of every stripe were concentrated in a small area around the campus. I'd never seen anything like this before, but it sure looked like party time to me!

For the first few months, I wandered about in a generally bewildered state of mind. Everything seemed so strange and overwhelming. Overnight, I was exposed to children of well-to-do white and black Americans, and I didn't have the social skills to communicate with them. I only knew how to deal with people who could *"walk the walk"* and *"talk the talk"* of the ghetto. The Italian community of Newark had its own style, which I had come to understand, so they were a special exception. But here, I felt like I was from a different country. With all my adolescent insecurities thrown in, I became totally confused and miserable.

I fell right in with other kids who were miserable and doing drugs in the privacy of their rooms. Nodding out in front the boob-tube tuned to late-night B-movies was a favorite pastime for a lot of them. My mind was still in the projects, and I would surely have gone down that dark hole of helplessness and desolation if it hadn't been for fencing. I clung desperately to it because I couldn't relate to anything else. My fencing classes were a haven of sanity amidst the chaos. I hugged and caressed my sabre because it had brought me this far. It was the only positive force in my life. It kept me from spending all my time doing drugs and hanging out with the wrong people. It gave me goals and a sense of accomplishment and self-worth. It was also the only thing I really enjoyed.

NYU was a powerhouse in the world of college fencing, just as Essex was in the high school arena. I'd heard about the caliber of the program before I arrived, but when I saw it for myself I was blown away. There were so many superstars there, it was like a fencing dynasty. I felt honored and awed and afraid to be among them. There were the coaches, Hugo Castello and his brother Jimmy, sons of the renowned Argentinian fencer Julio Castello. And there were student fencers like Ed Ballinger, Ruth White, and Steve Kaplan, who had already made the Olympic team. Seeing so much talent all in one place quickly raised my level of ambition. I realized that back at Essex, I might have been the best fencer around, but I was like a big fish in a little pond. NYU was like a tributary that led out into the great ocean—you could get there from here.

While I knew where I wanted to go with my fencing, my course of study was another matter. I had initially enrolled in NYU's School of Education because it was one of the easiest programs to get into. I soon discovered, however, that I was petrified of speaking in front of people. I thought, *What am I doing here? How can I possibly be a teacher? I can't stand in front of a bunch of people and look them in the eyes and convey a message! No way—I can't do it—I have to get out.* I thought, *Let me go into business. I'll do a lot of paperwork and I won't have to spend too much time with people.* So I transferred from the School of Education to the School of Business. What naiveté. What I didn't realize was that in business, you have to do the same thing, only on a higher level! Teaching kids is *much* easier than communicating with business people. But I ran from it because I was afraid. Little did I know that I was headed for a career with high-powered people, tons of money, and endless interaction.

Around the same time, I had a girlfriend who suggested that we go into therapy together. We were arguing a lot and not being totally honest with each other. Although we were living together, I felt that our relationship wasn't going anywhere. Still, I had my doubts about therapy. My immediate reaction was, "Why? So you think we're crazy?" She told me that some friends of hers went for counseling and said it really helped. I figured we had nothing to lose and agreed to give it a try.

Being introduced to Mildred Klingman, a dynamic Jewish New Yorker who conducted group therapy sessions in her spacious Upper West Side apartment, turned out to be the other lucky circumstance that saved my life. It was only after I started seeing her that I was able to begin dealing with my social development. After my girlfriend and I had our first private session, Dr. Klingman said that she wanted me to attend her group sessions. She felt I could get more out of group therapy, and said that she wouldn't charge me anything for it. When I insisted that I should pay *something*, she asked me what I could afford, and when I said five dollars she agreed.

I attended Dr. Klingman's group sessions twice a week. Most of the other people—there were about ten of us—were doctors, lawyers, and other highly educated professionals who paid ninety dollars a session. I was the only African American. The sessions involved facing our emotions and talking about them on every level you can imagine. The process taught me how to be honest with my feelings and how to articulate them. Some of the people seemed uncomfortable with the therapy process, but I took to it quite naturally. I knew I was getting better, and I enjoyed that. Very quickly I started benefiting in a way that was obvious to Dr. Klingman, who seemed especially happy to have me around—perhaps because my enthusiasm and bluntness contrasted so sharply with the somewhat muddled emotions of most of the other participants.

By the end of the first term, I felt I had learned all that I needed to. I was losing my fears and inhibitions and was learning how to "read" people and communicate with them. Rather than settling into the security of a familiar reality, I was learning to be open to new experiences and not to pre-judge situations before they unfold. I was convinced that I could go out in the world with confidence and apply the techniques I had learned. Dr. Klingman agreed, but asked me to stay and help her conduct the sessions. I was happy to comply.

I continued my therapy with Mildred Klingman throughout the '70s, and when I finally "graduated," I felt like I had earned a second college degree. That's how important those years of therapy were to me. I still see Dr. Klingman from time to time just to visit. I bring her a gift and stop by to say thanks. Sometimes she cries for joy when she sees me. Mildred Klingman is a doctor with a heart of gold. She was able to discover my needs and insecurities, hold them gingerly in her hand so I could see them, and point me in the right direction. She is one of the great inspirations of my life. She led me out of the dark ages, taught me to understand my mind, and helped me to grow by leaps and bounds. I owe her so much.

Every serious fencer has to have a fencing mentor, a personal coach. The form can only be perfected through countless hours of one-on-one training. I was getting better at fencing, and the coaches at NYU, seeing my potential, suggested that I start training with Csaba Elthes, a Hungarian sabrist at the New York Fencers Club who had a reputation as the best coach in the country.

I began studying with Csaba in 1972, during my junior year. When we met for the first time, I remember thinking, *Boy, this is one weird-looking man. He's got these scary Dracula eyebrows, he talks like Dracula, he even comes from the same part of the world as Dracula!* It didn't take long for me to discover that his teaching method was equally scary. Csaba's English was lousy, his language was foul, and he let out a constant stream of verbal and emotional abuse.

"You're nothing. You're a big zero. You're a piece of shit. You should flush yourself down the toilet."

He hurled these very words at me, all in a single breath, over and over again. To top it off, he'd whack me with his sabre every time I made a mistake.

Csaba's physical abuse was simply unacceptable to me. He actually believed that he could weed out mistakes by inflicting pain on that part of the body that was making the mistake! He'd say, "If you can't take this from an old man like me, you might as well quit." Born in 1908, Csaba Elthes was a sabre champion, cavalry officer, attorney, and career diplomat who had escaped to the U. S. in 1956 during the Hungarian Revolution. Csaba may have been old, but he was still very strong. It wasn't uncommon for his students to come out of their lessons bleeding. All my life I had seen husbands beating up their wives, brothers beating up brothers, and had witnessed cold-blooded murders in the streets; I couldn't see paying someone to beat me with a sword and a lashing tongue. Of course, Csaba had no idea that because I had seen so much physical abuse as a child, I had zero tolerance for that type of punishment. We weren't communicating. So after a semester with him, I quit.

I continued my fencing at NYU, and still had the ambition to rise to the championship level. NYU's fencers were known nationwide because we hadn't lost a duel meet in years. It was like playing with a whole teamful of Michael Jordans— we won *all the time*. Outside tournaments were a breeze for us, but fencing inside with my teammates was another story. There were so many egotistical young maniacs on the team that practice was very difficult, and plenty of bouts ended in arguments. Great athletes are always maniacs. They're always in denial. They'll say you didn't hit them when there's no question that you did. I remember sparring with great players like Steve Kaplan and Tom Sheridan. First we'd argue over who got hit, then we'd argue over the fact that we were arguing. Sometimes we'd whack each other with our swords as hard as we could, actually trying to do the other guy harm. But we'd always posture, pretending to be gentlemen fencers, and finish off our misdeeds with a "Pardon me."

In 1973, I finally hit the jackpot: I won the NCAA championship. The best college sabrist in the country—my first big title. My semester with Csaba had definitely helped. In truth, my skills had gotten so good that it wasn't so difficult for me to win. In fact, my coaches expected it of me. And whenever I won, it felt *sooo* good. I said, *I gotta keep going back to get more of this! Mmm hmm!* Winning is as addictive as any drug.

After speaking with a lot of people about my goals and my experiences with Csaba, it became clear that there was nobody else around who could put me on the U. S. Olympic team. So a year after walking out of my lessons at the New York Fencers Club, I returned to Csaba and begged him to take me back.

"I would like to start with you again, Sir."

"Fine," he agreed.

Csaba never hit me again. I realized that he understood when he said, "You're very intelligent; I don't have to do that to you. You *do* listen to what I say."

I said, "That's what I was trying to tell you before. Tell me once and I won't forget. I'm like a sponge. All you have to do is to tell me what I'm doing wrong."

Consequently, while everybody else in the country who trained with Csaba received hard whacks on their legs, to the best of my knowledge I was the only student that didn't get hit.

Csaba had me training seven days a week, from 4 in the afternoon until 9 or 10 at night. We'd start with a one-hour lesson, followed by footwork practice. Then I'd spar with other fencers, simulating competitive matches. I'd play against as many other fencers as I could to develop my reflexes and to hone my instinct for knowing what approach to use in any given situation. For instance, I'm a very quick fencer, but if my opponent is faster than I am (and there's always someone who is), I use my technique to slow him down or immobilize him. Once I gain the advantage, the tables turn, and I can use my speed against him. Or say my opponent is bigger and stronger than I am. I summon my courage not be intimidated by him, and then use my technique to parry (block) his big swings. I see if I can break him by hitting him softly or if I have to use all my might. I learned that some people only like to attack, and some only like to defend. If I'm up against an attacker, I close the distance between us to maximize my advantage. If I'm up against a defensive player, I try to throw him by attacking him with a variety of moves.

Csaba believed in me and worked me like a dog. This old world maestro put me on the road to championship fencing. Under his guidance, it wasn't long before I was reputed to be one of the best sabrists in the country.

MY LUCKY THIRTEEN

3

I am one of the best in the class with the broadsword. It is lots of fun...The other day I was fencing with a man who would not acknowledge my touches though they nearly knocked him down, so I tried a dueling cut...As a result he could not hold a pen for a day but will probably be a better sport in the future.
—General George S. Patton, as a West Point senior, in a letter written to his father

In 1974, as a college senior, I entered the Amateur Fencers League of America's* National Championships. I was nervous as hell. I had attended the Nationals a couple of times before, but it was only for practice. This time, my coaches had serious expectations of me.

The tournament was held at the Hotel Commodore near Grand Central Station in New York. I felt like I was running a marathon. It was like an endurance test to see who could

*Now known as the United States Fencing Association

fence match after match for ten hours straight and still perform their best. The competition was tough. There were world-class fencers like Alex Orban and Paul Apostol, both of whom were students of Csaba's, and many of the competitors from the 1972 Olympic team. Incredibly enough, none of these people were able to beat me.

Winning the Nationals suddenly made me the best sabrist America had. I thought, *This is impossible! How can this be true?* The idea left me dumbfounded. It was inconceivable to me to be in that position. Seven years after I'd first picked up a sabre, I became the first African American and one of the youngest people ever to win the national title in sabre fencing. I had no idea how to handle that kind of honor. For weeks I walked around in a daze until I finally calmed down enough to believe and accept it. Csaba certainly didn't expect it to happen either, at least not so soon. It was unnatural. Csaba felt it was dangerously fast. He was concerned that I didn't have the emotional maturity to deal with the title, and warned me not to let it go to my head.

"You can be a killer on the fencing strip," Csaba said, "but you must never let yourself be arrogant."

He explained to me that I was competing in a tough and highly politicized environment, and that I'd better make sure I was well-liked by those in power. Since sabre had not yet been electrified, the scores were based on the subjective calls of a panel of judges. So I not only had to make the most touches, I also had to make sure those white judges would raise their hands for me!

I appreciated Csaba's concerns, but I was on the big-time circuit now, and nothing was going to stop me. When the

1975 Nationals rolled around, I had to prove to everybody that I could do it again. And I did. It was the beginning of my unprecedented reign as U. S. sabre champion, a title I have won thirteen times—my lucky thirteen.

In 1975, I also brought home a silver team medal and a bronze individual from the Pan American Games in Mexico City. I was just a touch away from winning a gold. I was tied for first place with two Cubans, Manuel Ortiz and R. Salvador Guzman, so we went into the fencing equivalent of overtime. We had a three-way fence-off, and I got the bad end of a bad call. Everybody knew it. The Italian judge who was officiating the match was notoriously unfair. I was really broken by the loss. Csaba was depressed too, but he did his best to build me back up again.

Back in the U. S., I was under the mistaken impression that the title of national champion was mine for good. I thought I owned it. I didn't realize that it was only on loan. It's a gift you get when you're young. You can hold it for a fleeting moment, and then you must pass it on. In 1976, I lost my title. I came in second, but second was nothing to me. Absolutely nothing. I felt utterly worthless until the next year came around—and then I lost *again*. The guy that beat me both years was a Hungarian-American student from Columbia University named Tom Losonczy. Tom was also a student of Csaba's, and he had been training with him much longer than I had. What made the loss even more painful was when I realized that Csaba, who was like a father to me, was rooting for somebody else. Csaba wanted Tom to win. That hurt me tremendously.

These years were an agonizing time for me. I felt like I was nothing. I felt like dirt. I was so ashamed, I was almost dysfunctional. I needed to win just to feel adequate. I couldn't stand the feeling of inferiority that losing left me with. I defined myself strictly by my results. I couldn't distinguish myself as a person apart from my title, "Peter Westbrook, Best Fencer in the Country." I also assumed that because I had achieved this title, I had all the skills I needed down pat. What I didn't understand at the time was that I was being chased by demons. I was constantly running from my feelings of inadequacy, trying not to let them catch up to me. That came from growing up black and poor in America. The only thing that I knew would save me was winning these tournaments. I used my awards like camouflage so I wouldn't have to look at reality. And I used up my energy running away from these bad feelings.

By 1976, I was headed to Montreal for my first Olympic Games. At the pre-Olympic trials, I had placed number two in the world, right behind the powerful Russian Vladimir Nazlymov. Nazlymov was an extraordinary fencer with many world and Olympic titles to his credit. All the Europeans were wondering, "Who is this young black American fencer? How could he have such audacity?" Earlier that year, I had also beaten several top Europeans, including the Italian champion Mario Aldo Montano, and came in first place at the Martini & Rossi International Fencing Challenge. When it came time for the Olympic Games, the whole world was watching me.

When I arrived in Montreal, I was a jumble of emotions. I was in awe of the great event, blown away by all the superstar athletes there, and scared that I wouldn't be able to perform under all the pressure. Somehow I just didn't feel that

I belonged. I didn't feel like the great fencer that everyone seemed to believe me to be. After all, Americans have never been a force in the international fencing arena, so why should anything be different for me? There I was, about to compete against the prime physical specimens of every nation, and people were expecting me to be the best? It was too much for me to handle. I felt as miserable as a ten-year-old child who had lost his parents in the Olympic Village. I sure didn't feel like I was twenty-four.

Before my event, a number of world champions came up to me and asked if I would spar with them. They wanted to get a read on me to see how good I was. It dawned on me, *My God, I must be good. The world is actually afraid of me.* But the message refused to sink in. Then, four days before my first match, while I was practicing with one of the Europeans, I sprained my left ankle. I could barely walk. The ankle swelled up like a grapefruit. The doctors told me, "There's no way you're going to compete." I had torn two ligaments before my first Olympic Games.

In a way, the incident was a blessing. It took a lot of pressure off me. I still had every intention of competing, but if I didn't perform as well as everyone was expecting me to, I could blame it on my ankle. When I thought of how badly I felt after losing the national title and having to wait a whole year to prove myself again, I couldn't bear to think of how awful it would be to lose at the Olympics and to be stuck with that feeling for four more years. The anxiety and the stress made me desperate for a fallback. The ankle injury gave me a way out, a perfect excuse.

Again, I was not the only student of Csaba's at the competitions. In fact, every single member of the five-person U. S. sabre team had studied with the maestro. Csaba was so renowned for his extraordinary coaching that the Hungarians were trying to lure him back. Sometimes he would threaten to leave us, saying, "I am a big shit. What am I doing, staying here in America with the stupid people?" But in Montreal, Csaba's stupid people didn't do so badly. The team placed seventh, with Paul Apostol and me coming in as the top two American sabrists, and among the world's best, I managed to come in thirteenth. I didn't need to use my injury as a fallback after all; I was pleased with my results.

After Montreal, I competed in a number of European tournaments against the best fencers in the world. When I came out on top again and again, I saw that I really did have the skills, and finally began to feel I belonged. My confidence came back full blast. Ironically, my teammates came up with an odd nickname for me. They would say, "Man, Pete, you're the best thing we've got going in fencing. You're 'The Great White Hope.'" When I'd object to the "white" part, they'd say, "But it's true. You're *our* great hope."

In 1979, I won back the national title against Phil Reilly and the incredible Alex Orban. Once I regained that beloved title, I held on to it as tight as I could. I kept it for an unprecedented eight years running. By 1982, Alex and I had both accumulated a record five titles each, and the entire fencing world was at the edge of their seats waiting to see who would break the record. The following year at the Nationals in Washington, D. C., I broke the tie with my sixth win.

When President Carter boycotted the 1980 Olympics in Moscow to protest the Soviet invasion of Afghanistan, many American athletes were really furious. For a lot of them, their only chance to compete in the Olympic Games had just been dashed. But I wasn't concerned. I was so strong in 1980 that I knew I'd be back again in 1984. I felt there was no one better in the whole country. And I wasn't thrilled with the idea of spending three weeks in Moscow, anyway. I'd been there before and found it kind of dark and gloomy—not enough colors or smiles. I was happy with the alternate plan: we would go to China instead.

Traveling to China was the opportunity of a lifetime. China was a world of mystery to me, a forbidden land of silk and fireworks that had only recently been opened up to the Western world. But nothing I had heard or imagined prepared me for the radically different cultural experience that awaited us there. Throughout China, we encountered people who had never seen humans with black skin or blond hair. When we arrived in a town, mobs of people would run after us, trying to touch our skin and hair to see if the color would rub off.

I was also amazed by the honesty and generosity of the Chinese. At our hotels, we were never issued room keys. In fact, we were told to leave our doors open. Nothing was ever stolen. And tipping was not accepted, even covertly. Another curiosity I noticed was the clothing that the children wore. It was a freezing November, and all the kids were bundled up in snowsuits like little Eskimos. But the backs of their outfits had cutouts, leaving their behinds fully exposed. "For convenience," we were later told.

We spent three weeks traveling through four of China's provinces, competing against the country's top teams. As it turned out, I was the only American fencer who went undefeated in our competitions there. I was flying high from my streak of successes. I had come a long way since my first international tournaments four years before. Therapy, fencing, and the accumulation of life experience had made me stronger as an athlete and a person. But deep down, I knew that I was not at peace. I was still being haunted by the inferiority demon. At the time, I was so busy chasing after those wins that I never stepped back to analyze the madness behind my obsession.

Fencing had literally become a way of life for me. At any given moment, fencing was foremost on my mind. It scares me now to think about how deeply engrossed I was in the sport. I dreamed only about fencing. I'd wake up in the morning with my arms and hands going through the motions. Mentally, physically, and psychologically, I was constantly preoccupied with some aspect of fencing. Nothing else engaged me: not women, and not whatever job I had at the time. Any activity I participated in, whether it was with people or things, appeared to me as if it were a situation in a fencing match. I can't stress this enough. I had one objective only: to win.

If I'm fencing with you, my whole heart and soul is concerned with, *How can I do this gracefully and effortlessly?* I absorb your body language the way a dry sponge absorbs water. My objective is to get to know how you think, to anticipate your next move. I try to become aware of your slightest weaknesses, the ones you don't even know you have. Then I capitalize on them. That's how I can defeat you. I think this ability to put my body and heart and mind into another person's—to almost *become* them—is a gift from God. I was blessed with the right conditions to be able to use it. Having grown up on the tough side of the tracks, I have no qualms about preying upon the weaknesses of my enemies until they are no longer a threat to me. To do this in life is a crime, but to do it in the sport of fencing is to create beauty and art. It's all about negative manipulation and emotional intimidation. With each opponent, I immediately try to gauge, *How weak is this man? How many times will I have to beat him down in order to shatter him?* I try to think beyond a single match. I ask, *Can I scare him so bad that he'll bow down to me forever? How can I keep him as my prisoner for life?* I don't think that people who've grown up in mainstream society know how to do this. I definitely have an advantage in this regard. But it also takes an incredible amount of training and practice to fence consistently at this level. This is the kind of "inner fencing" that I learned to master. It gave me the sharp focus that opened doors in other areas of my life.

With my college training in business administration, I embarked on a marketing career selling computers for IBM. Working for IBM was a rude awakening. The company sent a group of us down to Atlanta to familiarize us with IBM's corporate culture. At the meetings in Atlanta, I discovered the heart of racism. My white co-workers' attitudes made me think that I had the Bubonic plague. When it became clear to me that they were really looking down on us blacks, I summoned the pride my mother had instilled in me and I became more arrogant and combative. I wasn't about to let anyone think they were superior to me. I soon found that I was fighting the whole world: fighting people in corporate America, fighting people close to me, and worst of all, fighting myself. While I had become aware of my combative tendencies during my years of therapy, I still hadn't learned how to harness my anger.

Three years later I was out of IBM. I spent the next year at Pitney Bowes, and then got a job making cold calls at North American Van Lines. I worked there for eleven years as their only African-American rep. During all my years of work, fencing remained my number one passion. Every day, as soon as the clock struck five, I would literally run to the club to train.

People around me seemed convinced that I had it all. Fencing had given me confidence and discipline. People have always been attracted to me, and with my gift for gab and minor celebrity status, I had plenty of relationships. And on the job, I was making more money than I could possibly spend. But I knew that something was missing. I realized that in the larger scheme of things, what I had was nothing. When I looked at these huge corporations, I saw that I was insignificant and replaceable. I was accumulating more and more money, relationships, titles on the job, titles in the fencing world, but I saw that none of this was going to make me a complete person in life. Then a truer reality started to reveal itself to me. I saw that success does not determine who you are. I don't know if most people really understand this. I don't think they do. I wasn't able to figure it out until I got all these things and was living on top of the world. What really impresses me is people who are able to figure it out before they get all these things. I don't know too many people like that.

The realization sent me into a bit of a panic. I felt lost. I thought, *If this is not what life's all about, then what am I doing here?* From that point forward, the search was on. I read countless books on philosophy, psychology, and spirituality, I took various New Age and human potential-style courses, I looked within myself and spoke to others who were doing the same. Being the doubting Thomas that I am, I always tested new ideas, putting them into practice in my own life to see if they would actually work for me. There was no single path that I chose to follow. Instead, I took bits and pieces of what I gathered from many sources and put them together in my own way. I had undertaken a lifelong quest for knowledge that would, in time, lead me to what I was searching for.

At the 1983 Pan American Games in Caracas, Venezuela, I was up against a big black Cuban who was strong as hell. He had played pro-baseball for his country, and could easily have been a heavyweight boxer as well. His name was Manuel Ortiz, and in 1975 and 1979, he had won the Pan American gold. Everybody was scared of him. My coach and I both knew that I had the skills to beat him, but we didn't know if I had the courage. Then I caught Montezuma's Revenge. Everyone had told me, "Pete, whatever you do, don't drink the water." I didn't, but I did use the tap water to brush my teeth and rinse my mouth. I had no idea that it was the same thing. Well, I caught that revenge so bad that I had to stay in bed. Deep down though, I knew it was blessing. I had another excuse. If I didn't perform well and didn't win a gold medal, I could blame it on Montezuma's Revenge. The pressure was off.

Unlike my situation in Montreal, however, this time the excuse made me more bold and daring. When I got on the strip for my final match, I felt I had nothing to lose. The Cuban was immediately on the attack. He was pure muscle, and he was hitting me with all his might. I'd never felt anything like it before. He was hurting me so bad that several times I almost buckled. I decided to try something ridiculous. I used a defensive motion. The next time Ortiz came at me, I blocked his weapon and made a riposte, or counterattack. The sequence I used is known as a quarte parry. Most of the time, you can get maybe two quarte parries in a bout. In those days, a bout was only ten touches. I did eight of these touches in a row! It took a lot of chutzpah to do that. But I kept on doin' it, and I won. I broke him. This invincible Cuban. It was a huge upset for the Latin Americans. I had won the war and would bring home a Pan American gold.

ON TOP OF THE WORLD

4

The odds of winning at the Olympics have always been stacked high against American fencers. Many people are not aware of the fact that in most other competing countries Olympic fencers are strictly professionals. Generous salaries, special privileges, media attention, and other perks are lavished on them —in the same way that basketball, football, and baseball players are treated in the United States. In France, for instance, two-time Olympic fencing champion Jean-François Lamour was recently named Athlete of the Year, with all the glamour and glory that accompanies such an honor. In stark contrast, America's Olympic fencers are amateurs who hold down outside jobs, train in their spare time, and pay coaches out of their own pockets. Sadly, fencing has never caught on as a spectator sport here, and it has been next to impossible to find long-term corporate sponsors for individual fencers.

Therefore, I was grateful to have the advantage of competing in my home country during the 1984 Olympics. Being in America meant that four thousand people in the audience would be rooting for me and calling out my name. I also had a psychological advantage. I had finally evolved enough to know that I didn't need to win just to feel adequate. I had worked through these problems in myself. I knew that even if I didn't come away with a medal, I wouldn't feel inferior.

When I walk onto the strip in Los Angeles for my final match against the Frenchman Hervé Granger-Veron, my adrenaline is pumping. One of us will receive a bronze medal, and I don't know if I can pull it off. Once again, I twist my left ankle during practice shortly before the Games. But I'm not looking for excuses anymore. This time I am fully prepared. I can conjure up all my strength and skills, all the emotional and intellectual and spiritual tools I have, and use them in a positive manner, without fear.

As the match begins, I get the first touch. I get the second touch. I make it to four. My touches appear to me to be so skillful, so beautiful, that I say to myself, *I think I'm in the Zone, but I'm not sure. Let me not think about it.* A lot of athletes and psychologists talk about this peak performance level called "the Zone." I think of the Zone as a spiritual gift that allows me to operate on an almost supernatural level and to produce incredible results. I don't like to tell myself I'm in the Zone too quickly, because you can easily find out that you're not a hundredth of a second later—when you lose.

Sure enough, as soon as the thought crosses my mind, the Frenchman gets two points on me. But I snatch the game right back. Soon the score hits 5-2, 6-2, 7-2, and I realize for sure that I'm in the Zone. Now I know I can do anything, and anything will work. Still, the battle isn't over.

In 1984, sabre was still not electrified. Today, when you hit your opponent, a light goes on, but in those days I had to count on a European judge to raise his hand for me. Just think about that. When I hit this Frenchman, the Europeans officiating are his *friends*. They do not want to give the point to me. But I've learned over time not to let the judges' calls break my spirit. So when I hit the guy once, twice, and no hand goes up, I know I gotta do it four, five, six more times before that hand begrudgingly rises. I get another touch, and it's 8-2. Then he gets 8-3, and 8-4. Even as he is gaining, I know the game is mine. All I gotta do is keep riding the tide, keep going with it. I get 9-4, and I finish him off 10-4. The Frenchman falls to his knees crying.

Ten years after my first Olympics, I had finally learned how to work in the Zone. On that day, I was able to realize it, to feel it, to understand it, and to run with it. I capitalized on that supernatural feeling. The Frenchman was devastated and the audience was amazed. When I looked out at the crowd, I could see that the Hungarians, the Italians, and the rest of the Europeans had all turned around. They went from not wanting my win to happen, to being forced to say in their hearts and souls, *Bravo. Bravo.* That, to me, was incredible.

I had won a bronze medal for myself, my teammates, and my country. But I realized later, and Csaba confirmed, that I could have won the gold. The match before my bout with Granger-Veron was with another Frenchman. His name was Jean-François Lamour, and he was the best fencer that France had produced in decades. Lamour beat me 10-5 and went on to beat an Italian named Marco Marin. Marin took the silver and Lamour took the gold. Lamour's Olympic performances were impressive all around. He didn't lose a single bout in Los Angeles, and would go on to win the gold again in '88 (and in '92, the bronze). But when I thought about my match with Lamour and watched it on videotape, I realized that I had a distinct advantage over my opponent: Lamour was really scared of me! He was more scared of me than I was of him, but at the time, I thought it was the other way around. And that was what determined who won.

The reason Lamour was so scared was because he had seen my previous match the day before. In order to get to the medal match with Lamour, I had to beat this Italian guy, Gianfranco Dalla Barba. I was fencing beautifully during that match, definitely a Zone performance, but the European official who was judging it was clearly biased. He screwed me out of seven touches in a row! It seemed like there was nothing I could do to win. I was not going to get past that match. A lot of people lose their wits in this environment. All those years of training, and in a single moment, there goes your match, there goes your Olympics, there goes your career. It's not fair, it's not right, but that's how it is. I knew I could use these unfair calls as an excuse, but I wasn't about to take them lying down. So in the middle of the match with the Italian,

I took off my mask and my gloves, I threw them on the ground, and I said, "I quit!"

The official pulled me aside. Gritting his teeth, he muttered, "Listen, Westbrook. I'll give you one more chance. If you don't pick up your gear and finish this match, you don't have to worry about quitting, because I'm going to throw you out of the Olympic Games!"

I held firm and said it again: "I quit." Then I fired the only bullet I had left in my gun. "I'm not going to stand here and let you cheat me in front of America and in front of the world."

Csaba and my teammates were appalled. They pleaded with me to calm down. They were convinced that I had lost my cool and was throwing away all that I had worked for. What they didn't realize was that this was a calculated plan in my mind. I was only bullshitting. I looked at Csaba and winked at him, meaning, *I've got this totally under control. I'm not going to quit, I'm just going to call his bluff.* I wanted to bring the whole world over to my side, and to bring these score-keeping shenanigans out in the open. I wanted to lay some heavy external pressure on that official—not to give me a break, just to call it fair. I dragged out my ploy for as long as I could, and finally returned to the strip.

At this point the score was 7-1. Dalla Barba only needed three more touches to win. I would say my odds were impossible. Definitely impossible. But I won. The truth was given back to me right then and there. All that praying and mental preparation I had done before the games paid off. The following day, I was the talk of the town. My name became so popular that everybody thought I would win the gold. So when I came out to fence the medal match against Jean-François Lamour, he was scared of me and so was the world. If only I had known!

The moment they placed the Olympic Bronze Medal around my neck as I stood on the champion's podium, I was beaming with pride. It was the crowning glory of all my years of training. Suddenly, I was famous—or as famous as a fencer in America can be. It was the most exhilarating and spectacular feeling I've ever had. Four thousand people were cheering for me. I was on top of the world. Long after the applause has subsided, the record of that win will remain, and will outlast me.

Since the first contemporary Olympic Games in 1896, the United States had only won four medals in fencing. At the 1904 Olympics in St. Louis, sabrist William Grebe won a silver and sabrist Albertson Van Zo Post won a bronze. At the 1948 Games in London, the U. S. sabre team took a bronze. And at the 1960 Games in Rome, foilist Albert Axelrod won a bronze. My win at the 1984 Olympics was the first for an American fencer in twenty-four years, and in my event, the individual sabre, in eighty years. It was America's fifth fencing medal, and the first for an African American.

Winning a medal in a sport dominated by Latin Americans and Europeans was not just a personal victory. I felt that I had won for all African Americans. I felt a tremendous pride for my people. Unfortunately, we still live in a social climate where if you are black or dark-skinned, you will encounter people who will hint or say outright that somehow you are not as capable as everybody else. Somehow you are disqualified from participating in things that most people take for granted. On that day, I proved those people to be dead wrong.

Winning also kindled in my chest a deep and abiding confidence in a higher spiritual reality. Whatever you choose to call that supreme power, God blessed me with the strength to face and to overcome many obstacles. Fencing allowed me to experience the kind of success, exhilaration, and satisfaction that were absent in all other aspects of my life. I realized that if I could win against professionals from all over the world, surely I could train my emotions and learn to meet challenges in any environment. Because the odds against my winning a medal at the Olympics were so great, I was convinced that I had been tapped on my head from above. It proved to me that I could be granted further blessings and strengths to deal with whatever other obstacles I should encounter.

At the 1987 Pan American Games in Indianapolis, everyone, myself included, thought I would win the gold. But my golden streak didn't last. I was fencing on a par with the Canadian Jean-Paul Banos, and in a tie-breaking finale, he beat me 12-11. Fortunately, I still managed to take home silver medals in the individual and team matches. I was disappointed to have lost my title, but this time, the disappointment didn't last long. I realized that I had won something else. For the first time, I found that I was no longer chasing after titles or living from one win to the next. My past victories and my spiritual pursuits had brought me to a new place. I had finally conquered my demons. I felt a sense of peace and contentment that I had never known before. At the end of the games, I was happy to say that I had fenced as well as I could, fought valiantly for my title, and come away with something even better than gold.

Nineteen eighty-seven was a year of discovery for me in another way as well. That summer I met a woman named Susann Miles. Susann was exactly what I needed. She has the kindness of an angel and the patience of a saint. Any normal person would not have been able to put up with my mad world of fencing, my all-consuming obsession. Susann is so easy-going that somehow she's managed to bear with all of the craziness as I've trained for three Olympic Games.

I know I may sound like a Neanderthal caveman, but I always say that women and sports don't mix. Let me explain it to you and maybe you'll see my point. When you're in competition and you have your love interest with you, you have two things to worry about. You have to wonder, _Is she okay? Is she having a good time?_ This uses up a little bit of your strength, your emotions, your intellect. When European athletes go away to training camps—and the same holds true for American boxers—their wives are not allowed. Sports is warfare, it's like going off to war. If I'm fighting in Vietnam or World War II and I gotta bring my wife with me, you better believe I'm going to be thinking of her welfare in addition to mine. That will not make me the best soldier. So when I say that women and sports don't mix, all I'm saying is that I can't help but care for my woman, and in a competitive situation, that takes away some of my power. This is not just a man thing, by the way.

I've spoken with a number of women athletes about this phenomenon, and they tell me it's also true for them.

At the 1988 Olympics in Seoul, the U. S. fencing team had a new look. For the first time, we had a major African-American contingent. There were five of us: foilists Peter Lewison and Sharon Monplaisir; my clubmates and soulmates, sabrists Mike Lofton and Bob Cottingham; and myself. The whole world would see that this elite white sport was not so white anymore!

Mike Lofton had started hanging around the New York Fencers Club in 1983. At that time, he was a skinny little high schooler with a big head—a real cute kid. He came to train with Csaba and me. We could see his talent right away, and I knew that pretty soon he'd be my enemy. Sure enough, he took the national title in '91 and '92. Bob also came to the club as a high school student. A New Jersey native, Bob is a big, strong man, a terrific physical specimen who could easily play any sport. When we first sparred, he was a wildman, all over the place. But I could see that he was destined for greatness. He snatched the national title straight from my hands in 1990.

Seoul was a great disappointment for me in terms of my individual results. I was up against a Russian when there was a bad call to my disadvantage. I was eliminated before the final rounds. I remember feeling grateful to have as many wins as I did behind me, because I knew that this kind of experience could cripple an athlete for life. And I was thankful that our team did well. We placed seventh.

In 1989, I made the finals in the world championships. In many ways this is a tougher competition than the Olympics, in terms of the number of serious fencers that attend and the number of top players that compete in the final matches. That year, there were eighty-nine sabrists competing, and at the age of thirty-seven, I was already the oldest one there. The event was an historic one, in that the sabre had finally been electrified. This meant that machines would now be the arbiters of whether or not a touch had been made. No one was happier than me to see the element of human bias in scorekeeping eliminated from the game.

My first victory came in an early round, when I won a bout with Jean-François Lamour and knocked him out of the competition. Lamour was the defending world champion as well as a two-time Olympic gold medalist. I went on to win matches against top-ranking fencers from Russia, Germany, and Italy. In the quarterfinals, I lost a bout to Jaroslaw Koniusz of Poland, who eventually placed second, while I came in eighth in the world. I was thrilled to have done so well. Though eighth place doesn't sound nearly as impressive as winning an Olympic medal, this was actually a greater victory for me. I had battled against the Soviet-bloc powerhouses who had boycotted the '84 Olympics, and I had become America's first world championship sabre finalist in thirty-one years.

When I entered the 1992 Olympics in Barcelona, I felt certain that this event would mark the end of my competitive career. My work at the Peter Westbrook Foundation was really taking off, my knees were creaking, and it seemed high time for me to lay down my sword and focus my energies elsewhere. The realist in me had already accepted the inevitable fact that I would not be going out with a bang. While I was thrilled to participate in my fifth Olympic Games and would certainly give it my all, neither I nor my sabre teammates expected to bring home any medals from Barcelona. We just didn't rank among the world's best that year. But our hopes were high for the women's fencing team. Any win would have been great for our sport, as with it comes the recognition that brings in the funding that keeps fencing alive. Unfortunately, none of us American fencers were able to strike it rich that year.

Nevertheless, Barcelona held some unexpected glories. I came away with a great sense of pride in knowing that not only had I witnessed the changing of the guard in my event, I had also been there to pass on what I could to my younger fencing brothers. I shared some wonderful moments with Bob Cottingham, in particular. During a match against a powerful Russian, Bob was in a bind. He was getting badly beaten and didn't know what to do. He finally called for a time-out and summoned me to the strip. Bob and I are so close and there is so much trust between us that I can pretty much imagine myself in his body. Feeling his fears and knowing his abilities, I stood nearby and called out his moves every step of the way. In the end, I literally walked him through to victory.

Bob and I knew a thing or two about playing together in this way because we had done it once before. At a European tournament that both of us had entered to win qualifying points for the Barcelona Games, Bob was fencing a Frenchman. At first Bob had the lead, but the Frenchman suddenly took hold of the game and got six touches in a row. Bob kept making the same mistake over and over again, only he didn't know it. Now the game was tied 9-9; whoever got the next touch would win. I called Bob over to the side and told him to try this trick: "Let the Frenchman push you to the very end of the strip, until he thinks you're going to step off. When I shout, 'Now!' you hit the guy on the head." Sure enough, our feint worked like a charm. When Bob was announced as the winner, the whole American team broke out in a roar of laughter.

My final moment of joy in Barcelona came at the closing ceremonies. There, I had the singular honor of carrying Old Glory, the stars and stripes of the United States, for our team. I was tremendously proud to represent my country in this manner, and deeply moved that my teammates nominated me and voted me in to be the standard-bearer for the most powerful country in the world. In fact, I couldn't imagine a more fitting way to leave what I assumed would be my final Olympic Games.

No matter what else happens during my competitive career, my Olympic medal will always be seen as the ultimate mark of glory. But I know that it is just a symbol. I like to think that I'd be the same person I am today even without that medal, but I don't know if that's true. Once you achieve this pinnacle, it totally changes your life. My Olympic victory gave me a feeling of success and accomplishment that I could transfer into other areas of my life. I know the skills and mentality it takes to have a winning attitude, and I know how to harness that attitude. It's not about feeling superior and putting people down, but about opening up to others and doing it in a humble way. Not too many people in the world are able to be the best at anything. To have this and to use it with humility is the most amazing feeling.

5

A BRIEF HISTORY OF FENCING

with Csaba Elthes

"*On-guard and admire what my valiant hands shall do!*"

This proclamation is not from *The Three Musketeers* or some other seventeenth-century-based adventure novel. Rather, it is from a much older source: an inscription found on the earliest record of a fencing match. It accompanies a relief carving that dates from around 1190 B. C. This ancient bas relief in the temple of Madinat Habu built by Ramses III near Luxor in upper Egypt depicts a practice bout or tournament. It is clearly not a battle or a duel because the points of the swords are covered. The parrying fencers are wearing masks tied to what appear to be their wigs or dreadlocks with padding over their ears, and are fitted with large bibs. They have narrow shields tied to their left arms. Judges and other officials carrying feathered wands stand in the background, along with spectators from nearby Syria and Sudan. Despite the minor differences in equipment and attire, there is something extraordinarily contemporary about this 3,000-year-old fencing scene. Virtually the only thing missing are today's "electronic judges"—the wiring rigged to the fencers' bodies and their weapons for accurate scorekeeping.

Most of us know almost nothing about the history of fencing or the way the game is actually played. In real life, fencing hardly resembles the Hollywood version of the sport made popular by swashbuckling heroes like Douglas Fairbanks and Errol Flynn in those old black-and-white movies. A guy fencing like that in a match today wouldn't last more than a few seconds.

How does one learn about fencing? When I started winning at tournaments, people would give me all sorts of books to read. I enjoyed reading the psychological books on subjects like self-mastery and the competitive edge, but the books on fencing and combat really didn't do anything for me. I learned my fencing by fencing, and by spending time with fencers. I was with top-notch fencers all the time. My coach constantly talked to me about fencing, tirelessly responding to every question I could possibly think of. One simply cannot master this sport without investing countless hours in one-on-one training. Csaba Elthes was like a *sensei* to me, my teacher. That's how important the trainer is in this sport. But knowing something about the history of the sport is also important.

Having some historical perspective satisfies our curiosity and helps us to see the sport in another light. There are many fascinating stories from the history of fencing. Sadly, they are not readily available in print. A few rare tomes about fencing are available in French, Italian, Spanish, and other languages, but little in English. I had the great good fortune of studying with someone who came from a time and place where fencing was king. Csaba Elthes inherited a rich oral tradition, and passed it on to his students. Fortunately, I managed to tape record some of the wonderful fencing lore that Csaba passed on to me:

"Fencing is one of the oldest martial sports. Stone-age people fenced. They were fighting each other with canes. What was fencing? Try to hit and kill the other. A deadly sport. The smarter one finds out that the cane can be used to protect as well as to hit. He learns how to parry and defend himself, and after that, to come back to deliver a blow where the opponent is unprotected. This is practically fencing. Many thousands of years later when metal was discovered, man made weapons that were more deadly. Roman gladiators fought each other to the death in front of thousands of spectators seated around them in a giant stadium. They used a variety of weapons and each event had its own set of rules. They wore some kind of armor to protect themselves. The quickest, strongest, and most artful fighters usually won.

"Later, in the Middle Ages, fencers wore still heavier armor to protect themselves. In fourteenth-century Europe, after traveling merchants brought back gunpowder from China, warfare began to be conducted on a much larger scale. Heavy armor became useless in the path of a red-hot iron cannonball. But for one-on-one combat, skillful swordplay was the name of the game and the art of fencing remained a deadly sport. Fencing required such discipline and agility that it was retained as a basic training method for soldiers and officers of all armies. It was a generally accepted fact that a good fencer was also competent in all other areas.

"In the fifteenth century, fencing masters started developing the art of swordsmanship. Kings and emperors granted them authority to form guilds. Within the structure of such institutions, fencing masters discovered new moves. These were generally kept secret, but were occasionally sold to wealthy pupils for large sums of money. Practiced and perfected in secrecy, these strategic sequences of advances, retreats, ripostes, feints, and lunges could be suddenly unleashed to surprise and fatally overwhelm an unsuspecting opponent.

"With the emergence of swordplay as a precise art form and discipline, important books on the subject came out in France, Italy, and Spain. Early fencing also incorporated wrestling. Coaches wrote about the rules and the basic forms and motions of their own fencing styles. They circulated these style manuals among their initiates. This was one way that fencing evolved. These books were also circulated in the military. Good fencing was a big advantage on the battlefield. The one who could best handle the weapons was the winner.

"Dueling is a dramatic aspect of fencing that has captured the whole world's attention. The mother of all combat sports, dueling with swords was a popular way of resolving differences all over Europe. Many colorful accounts of legendary duels utilizing masterfully executed strokes can be found in the European literature of the time. Dueling continued into the present century before it was outlawed.

"The duel has always had very strict rules. Fighting over women was considered a light affair. *Cherchez la femme.* Then duelists would use lighter sabres and tie bandages around vulnerable areas of the body for protection. Seldom did anyone die from such duels. However the more serious the conflict, a big political insult, for example, the less protection was allowed, and the incidence of death increased. It has been recorded that in France alone during the eighteen-year period between 1590 and 1608, some 8,000 people died dueling. They dueled without masks or bandages. Those were very dangerous conditions. One's honor was at stake and one was prepared to die defending it."

This is the kind of fencing lore that wafted like thick smoke through the schools and salons of Csaba's Budapest.

In the late sixteenth century, the Italians developed a style that emphasized the use of the point rather than the edge. Using a lighter weapon, the rapier, the emphasis shifted toward economy of movement and a more efficient use of the weapon. The Italians discovered the lunge. Wrestling was abandoned but the left hand still held a dagger and was protected by a gauntlet or cloak. Opponents circled around each other thrusting and avoiding by ducking *(passata sotto)* or sidestepping *(inquartata).*

In the early 1600s, the Spaniards developed their own game. They would move their feet on various lines drawn in a circle on the ground. They employed these moves with mathematical precision, a style the Italians never went for. Still, the Spanish technique anticipated the style to come out of the court of Louis XIV of France.

Towards the end of the seventeenth century, Louis XIV decreed that fashion ruled. Men, women, and children had to dress elaborately according to the dictates of the King's fashion designers. Men at court had to wear wigs, silk stockings, breaches, and brocaded coats. Both women and men donned coiffures on their heads and decorated their faces with layers of creams, paints, powders, and strategically placed beauty marks. Women's necklines plunged, while worldliness was cultivated by the ruling classes.

The revolution in style didn't stop at looks. It even affected the way people moved. Young courtiers had to execute complex dance steps to go through a regular day at the court, and had to carry a short court sword. This new weapon was not just a fashion accessory; proficiency with it soon became an indispensable skill for every gentleman. It could be used at close quarters. The dagger was no longer employed, so for the first time, the other hand was freed. Wrestling was abandoned completely. Chivalry and decorum were taken to great extremes during the reign of Louis the XIV.

As Csaba explains, "Fencing did not become a real sport until the end of the eighteenth century. In 1750 a French master named La Boessiere 'invented' the mask. It is a curious fact that it took so long for the mask to be used in Europe, since the Egyptians used it at least 2,000 years before. But now that there was protection of the exposed facial area, many schools opened where young people could study fencing as a sport. And once fencing was accepted in the academies, extensive 'conversations in swordplay'—the exchange

between two players of a distinctive repertoire of moves—
became possible within the framework of rules and conventions."

Long before my time, there were a number of famous black
fencers, particularly in France. By black, I mean those of us
with some amount of "black blood," which is how popular
opinion has always defined blacks. A more accurate definition might be those of us with the slightest trace of African
ancestry. While it is still a common practice in European
and Latin American countries to refer to the offspring of
mixed parentage—both white and non-white —as either
mulattos, people of color, or the derogatory "mixed
breeds," I myself think of these people, my brothers and sisters, as black.

In eighteenth-century France, there was a sizable population of *gens de couleur* (blacks of European ancestry). On the
eve of the French Revolution, when ideas of individual rights
and liberty were coming to the fore, there were many blacks
in Europe who were free men and women. Often they were
the offspring of titled aristocrats who had made their fortunes
in the New World. When these aristocrats retired from the
hectic life of wheeling and dealing in African slaves, a good
number of them wound up with attractive slave concubines
whom they later freed and married. Their children were
raised by their black mothers and European fathers. Unlike
in the States, where white fathers treated their own black sons
and daughters as slaves even if they were baptized, in several
great European nations, including France and in its colonies,

mixed offspring could enter into society, have certain privileges, and make their mark as free men and women. Although they faced tremendous prejudice, they enjoyed a social mobility that was not possible for blacks in the United States where, despite the Declaration of Independence, they were forbidden by law to receive an education.

Thomas-Alexandre was the favored son of a Frenchman who built his fortune in the French West Indian slave trade. Thomas's father, the Marquis de la Pailleterie, had sired three children with a Creole slave woman named Marie-Cessette Dumas. The Marquis had become attached to his son Thomas-Alexandre, and managed to bring him home to France.

During this time, it was common to see blacks among the ranks of King Louis XVI's armies. In fact, the Chevalier de Saint-Georges, a black French nobleman, was commissioned by the king to form a regiment composed entirely of men of color. When the French Revolution began in 1789, Thomas-Alexandre quickly enlisted in the army as a simple soldier. His father was outraged that his son was dragging his aristocratic name through the mud by being a low-rank foot soldier. He forbade his son to use his name. Thomas-Alexandre, who was already disappointed by the miserliness and distemper of his old father the Marquis, adopted the Dumas name from his mother. In 1792, he attained the rank of lieutenant colonel and married a French girl named Marie-Louise Labouret in the town of Villers-Cotterets. He went on to earn the rank of general and to become widely renowned for his military exploits.

The most famous of [Dumas's] exploits was probably his single-handed defense of the Bridge of Brixen, at Clausen in Austria, against an entire enemy squadron. As the bridge was narrow, only two or three men could confront him at a time, and Dumas sabered everyone who approached him. He was wounded three times and his coat was pierced by seven balls, but he stopped the enemy charge. The terrified Austrians nicknamed him "the black devil."

The color of his skin was also remarked on during the French invasion of Egypt: His brown color. . .resembling the Arabs, strongly impressed the garrison. Napoleon, who was in charge of the armies by then noticing this, sent for the mulatto general and ordered him to head the garrison vanguard intruding inland, so its members could see the skin of the very first general they had to deal with was not of an unfamiliar hue. *

As the war progressed, Napoleon's colonial army was devastated in Haiti by a mutiny and revolution led by the great black general Toussaint l'Ouverture, making Haiti the first free republic in the New World. It is well documented that Napoleon, a Corsican, later became distrustful toward blacks in his army. In fact, through trickery, he managed to capture Toussaint l'Ouverture, who died in prison in 1803.

*From the introduction to *Charles VII at the Home of His Great Vassals* by Alexandre Dumas, translated and with an introduction by Dorothy Trench-Bonett (Chicago: The Noble Press, 1991).

Napoleon also imprisoned General Dumas, under false pretexts. But the general survived his prison term and retired to Villers-Cotterets in 1801, where he and his wife raised two daughters and a son called Alexandre Dumas. Alexandre, born in 1803, had his own unique talents. He became a prolific and well-known writer, the author of such historical classics as *The Count of Monte Cristo* and *The Three Musketeers*. His autobiography documents a great deal about the realities of life in France for people of color. Thus we know of General Dumas's "swift series of promotions" leading up to his appointment as the head of a cavalry division during France's Italian Campaigns.

So, the legacy of the slave woman Marie-Cessette Dumas did not end with the mulatto general Thomas-Alexandre. Nor did it end with the general's son, Alexandre, the writer. For Alexandre Dumas (also known as Dumas *père)* had his own son, whom he named Alexandre Dumas (or Dumas *fils*), who went on to become a playwright and a darling of French society.

Against such a backdrop, the following story that Csaba Elthes used to tell us becomes even more revealing. Who was the greatest fencer that ever lived? While we in the U. S. know little or nothing about the hundreds of years of fencing history in Europe, Csaba grew up hearing stories about the great fencers of the past. In the European world of fencing, everyone had heard about the greatest fencer who ever was.

"Jean Louis was probably the greatest fencer who ever lived. He lived in the beginning of the nineteenth century under Napoleonic rule. His father, a fencing coach in the French army, was responsible for the fencing fitness of one thousand soldiers. Jean Louis's mother was a black woman from one of France's Caribbean or African colonies. In those days it was not uncommon for French sailors and soldiers to marry women of African ancestry and bring them back to France from their foreign colonies. Obviously, not looking like everybody else and being real minorities, blacks had to be outstandingly good in order to find acceptance and recognition in French society. Jean Louis was physically a cripple in his legs, but he loved fencing dearly. His father refused to teach him the sport, so secretly Jean Louis took lessons from a friend of his father's who was also a fencing coach in the same army. Jean Louis trained in secrecy until he achieved a perfect technique. Fate gave him a chance one day to demonstrate the power of his shocking accomplishment.

"Like his father, Jean Louis had become a fencing coach in Napoleon's army. During Napoleon's unsuccessful attempt to conquer Spain after having conquered practically all of Europe and Russia, his army consisted of French, Russian, Polish, German, and Italian divisions. An officer from one of the non-French divisions insulted an officer from the French division and challenged the French to a duel involving thirty people. Following the customs of such a duel, the officers in question were apparently exluded from the fighting. Instead, Jean Louis was chosen as the first man to take up this challenge. In what was to become the most legendary duel in fencing history, Jean Louis single-handedly defeated the first eight opponents one after another by mortally or heavily wounding them. After that stunning performance, the other twenty-two refused to fight him.

"In 1907, the French erected a life-sized statue of Jean Louis in the southern town of Montpellier as a memorial to his outstanding achievement. They honored him further by including his picture in every issue of the French fencing magazine, *L'Escrime*. Jean Louis looked very elegant in the picture, dressed in proper traditional fencing attire complete with gold accessories. That is the story of Jean Louis of France."

By the mid-nineteenth century, contests were being held regularly in France, Italy, Spain, parts of Germany, and Hungary. The Italians dominated sabre fencing and in general sabrists were accustomed to *wrist* fencing. Then the great Milanese fencing master Giuseppe Radaelli discovered *elbow* fencing, a style that made the sport more colorful. In 1896, a great international fencing tournament was held in Budapest, Hungary. This was *the* professional competition between the world's greatest fencing masters. The winner was an Italian named Italo Santelli. The Hungarians, who considered sabre to be their national sport, invited this Italian master to come to Budapest to teach them what this new elbow fencing style was all about. And so Italo Santelli came to Budapest, and until his death he taught the Hungarians the new style.

In the 1908 Olympics in London, Hungarian sabrists won the team and the individual gold medals. This event marked the beginning of the Hungarian domination of Olympic sabre fencing that lasted for fifty-six years. They had evolved the new dominant style, which was a combination of wrist and elbow fencing. The Hungarian dynasty was finally broken in 1964, when the mantle passed to the Russians.

After World War II, during the 1948 Olympic Games held in London, the Russians participated as observers. There they discovered, after having derided and outlawed fencing as a bourgeois sport, that a country could win a total of twenty-four different gold medals in fencing alone. Quickly, it was not so bourgeois anymore—they started seeing gold. So they took up fencing in a calculated and professional way. In the '50s the Russians came to Budapest to learn how to fence, and the Hungarians taught them. However, the Russians also had other plans that included some not so complimentary ideas about Hungarians. Soon after, they invaded Hungary and clamped down heavily on innumerable rights and freedoms.

The Russian invasion of Hungary led to a talent bonanza for the West. Some of the best Hungarian minds came to America. Csaba Elthes was one of them. Csaba was born in Budapest and emigrated to the U. S. in 1956 after getting fed up with the Communist regime. Csaba was a lawyer and diplomat by training, and the Russians had initially inducted him as a high-level government functionary. When Csaba arrived in America, he soon found out that most professional avenues were closed to him due to his foreign education and language. He would have to make a living as a fencing coach.

In his forty-year career, Csaba coached more champion fencers in the U. S. than anyone else. He was our revered teacher at the New York Fencers Club, and the trainer of most of the coaches at my foundation. Ever the perfectionist, he always tried to get the best out of us. If we had taken him too seriously we'd all have given up fencing a long time ago.

Csaba drank like a horse and smoked like a chimney. In 1980, he suffered a stroke which paralyzed his right hand. Incredibly, he managed to continue coaching with his left. And though he eventually regained the use of his fighting hand, it never fully recovered. However, this didn't stop him from being the very best coach in America. I was fortunate enough to have had eight years with Csaba when he was still in his prime. We would work together to create new, superfast, devastating moves. He put so much in my memory bank during those years, that I was able to draw from that store of knowledge for the rest of my career.

On the benefits of fencing, Csaba would say, "This is absolutely an individual sport. No other sport exists where the pupil and the coach have to be as close to each other as in fencing. Not boxing, not wrestling, nothing. Because in fencing, the coach has to *create* the fencer. This is true whether the student is talented or not. In the history of fencing, there have been many great fencers who weren't talented physically, but still became great fencers, even Olympic champions! The key elements are diligent practice and a very good coach. Close contact with the coach is essential in this sport to mold the character of the aspiring fencer.

"In Europe, fencing wasn't just a sport, it was an education. Here in the United States, somebody can learn a little fencing and start to teach. In Europe this would be considered a punishable crime. In Europe, you cannot teach fencing unless you have passed very rigorous exams to earn a fencing diploma. The benefits of such an education are enormous. Here even a masseur, for example, has to have a permit or diploma to give a massage. No such checks exist here for fencing teachers. But we are in America and not Europe.

"In Hungary, a great coach was not only a fencing coach but was also a professor of ethics and manners. His professional title was something like 'Fencing Coach, Professor of Excellent Manners, or Professor of Good Behavior.' They generally tended to be very well-educated people, if not always men with hereditary titles such as Count so-and-so. To this day, fencing is a compulsory sport at all the European military academies, presumably because they believe it to be a balanced discipline required to turn out responsible officers with good judgment.

"Fencing was even required at American military schools up until the 1950s, when it was phased out. That was a big let down for us coaches, as you can well imagine. What a pity. Therefore, while in some respects the fencing scene is very different here, the need for well-behaved, strong individuals is still very great. But strength of character can only be learned through close contact between pupil and coach.

"A good coach is like a sculptor. But coaching is more difficult because the sculptor creates a statue from inanimate material, while a fencing coach has to create a well-behaved, disciplined, self-controlled individual from a real person. There is a different mentality about the sport in Europe, which can be very difficult for Americans to understand.

"In fencing, quick thinking and self-control are a must. Simultaneously you have to learn good behavior and good manners. In Europe, the mood in a fencing room is similar to what you find in church. Undisturbed. Only individuals with permits can enter. Traditionally in Europe, the fencing room was a place where people protected their honor with blood. When I was young, every evening after 9:00 p.m. the fencing room would be open only to duelists. Understand? Fencing teaches not just self-confidence, but also courage. When you are engaged with an opponent you have to fence with ardor. Nobody can help you. You have step forward to fight for your honor *alone*. Do you understand what that means? A fencing coach has to help pupils learn what it is to be independent. The other great advantage of fencing besides self-confidence is discipline. Absolute discipline and absolute concentration. Both are extremely essential for living a good life. You need both.

"Like chess, fencing requires great mental agility. Perhaps that is why it was regarded as the 'first sport' of the Olympics—the pinnacle of athletic achievement—during the early Olympic Games. Presumably the other reason was that an overwhelming number of professional fencers in Europe came from the ranks of well-educated aristocrats. Therefore, a fencing coach had to be a very highly qualified and respectable person. In the old days, kings often conferred titles on fencing coaches. The United States has too many unqualified coaches, although of late, good Russians and Eastern Europeans have been coming to America. Without a good coach, it is impossible to make a really good fencer."

Csaba never failed to goad and challenge his students to do better than we ever imagined we could do. He kept us on our toes right up to his last days. This was his rare and special quality, and we will always remember him for it. Thanks to him we didn't do *too* badly. How lucky we are to have learned from one of the best in the world.

CLOSE SHAVES

You and your opponent are one. There is a coexisting relationship between you. You coexist with your opponent and become his complement, absorbing his attack and using his force to overcome him. —Bruce Lee

On April 1, 1992, my teammate Dave Mandell and I were fencing at the club. Dave kept falling for the same feint. Each time he advanced on me, I stuck my blade out and hit him on the chest. I was surprised when he fell for it the second time. Then the third. Mine was a simple deception, but each time he came back at me quicker and with more aggression. I could see that Dave was getting pretty upset. We were both assuming that the other wouldn't try the same move again, but each time we surprised each other. The only difference between us was that the tip of my sabre was striking his chest. When he came at me for the fourth time, I hoped he wouldn't think I'd do it again. I raised my elbow and stuck out my sabre. This time Dave was coming at me as fast as he could.

He impaled himself on the tip of my blade, and in total disbelief, he kept coming at me with the bent blade on his chest, until finally the tip broke off. I then tried to retreat as fast as I could, pulling on my weapon at the same time.

"I can't believe you got me with that same move again!" he said.

"I never thought you'd believe that I'd repeat the move again and again," I said, "because only an idiot would do that—or else a genius."

"I know, I'm the idiot."

"Well, I'm not saying that, but you fell for it four times in a row, which is quite a bit."

This whole exchange between Dave and me took place very quickly. When I finally glanced at the tip of my sabre, it looked like it had been dipped in red ink. I didn't tell him immediately because I didn't want him to get paranoid. I put my broken blade down and said, "Dave, my sabre punctured you."

"Nah, I feel fine."

"No, I think I punctured you. Open your jacket and see," I insisted.

When he opened his jacket, there on his white T-shirt was a red stain two inches in diameter. In another instant it had grown into a splotch ten inches in diameter.

When Dave saw *that*, he got dizzy and almost passed out. I brought him upstairs to the locker room and showed him my broken, blood-tipped blade and told him it had penetrated his flesh. At this point Dave, usually stoic and brave, started moaning and crying so loudly that people all over the club could hear him. He was acting like these were his last moments among the living.

"Peter, I can't breathe! I can't breathe!"

"No, Dave. You *can* breathe."

Dave started hyperventilating, and his face was turning white as a sheet. Meanwhile, there was a certain amount of deliberation among the people at the club before going to the hospital because Dave had no medical insurance. A medic who happened to be there told us that if we went straight to the emergency room, Dave would get attention the fastest, and they wouldn't ask questions about insurance until later.

Someone dialed 911. Soon the police arrived, along with an ambulance and several medics.

"All right, fellas, who's the guy that stabbed him?" The cops were immediately starting an investigation.

"I did," I volunteered.

"Why did you do it?"

"It was an accident, officer. We were practicing and the blade broke."

"Where is the weapon?" they demanded.

I showed them my sabre.

"We need this thing as evidence."

"That's my sabre. I need it." I tried to reason with them.

"No, no, we have to take this. So why'd you do it, buddy? Were you guys arguing?"

Somehow we just weren't getting through. Four or five times, a group of us from the club tried to explain to the cops that it was a freak accident, but they were still suspicious and unfriendly. We were not getting anywhere, and poor Dave

Mandell couldn't straighten things out because he was trying to get some air behind an oxygen mask. I tried once more. "Listen, just listen. You guys are not getting the point. We are Olympic fencers. We were practicing and my blade broke when I tried to hit him. It was not supposed to, but I think the blade has pierced his lung. This wasn't supposed to happen. Don't you get it?" That calmed them down.

When we got Dave to the emergency room, they found a punctured lung. The broken tip had penetrated about an inch-and-a-half. It was lucky that when I felt his body against my blade I started pulling back quickly. If I had advanced, it could have penetrated as much as seven inches. He could have died. Mind you, Dave was not wearing a Kevlar jacket, which were not in common use yet and would have prevented the injury. Nevertheless, he recovered fully.

Is fencing a dangerous sport? It's certainly a reasonable question, given what's at stake. With the protective jacket and armored mask that fencers are required to wear, there are far fewer injuries in fencing than in boxing, football, basketball, or hockey. The jackets worn today are made of the bulletproof material known as Kevlar and are strong enough to sustain a force of 800 newtons. The masks can resist up to 1,600 newtons. The examples of serious injuries I am giving here are very rare occurrences, and are in no way meant to dissuade people from taking up this sport. Statistically, more life-threatening accidents occur in everyday life than on the fencing strip.

Still, just as oriental martial artists demonstrate their power by chopping ten bricks with a bare hand, in fencing

My communion, at age seven.

My Japanese grandparents.

My mother enjoyed sports as
a girl in Kobe, Japan.

My mother as a young lady in Japan.

Vivian and me, all dressed up for church, in front of the Hayes Homes Projects.

My parents, Mariko and Ulysses Westbrook, young and in love.

My mother, my sister, and me, 1992.

Susann and me with Dorian after his graduation from
Arts & Humanities Junior High School, June 1993.

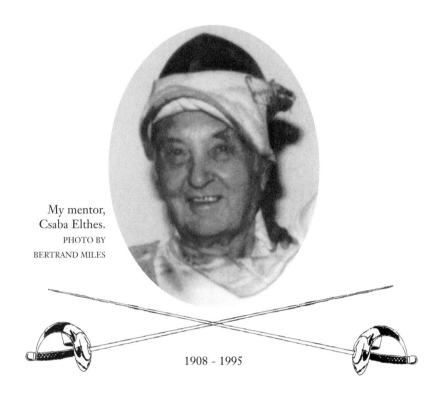

My mentor,
Csaba Elthes.
PHOTO BY
BERTRAND MILES

1908 - 1995

The foundation crew. Left to right: Csaba Elthes, Tom Shepard, Julia Jones, Eric Rosenberg, Aladar Kogler, Mike Lofton, Alpha Alexander, Bob Cottingham, me, Don Anthony, and Gerry Rodriguez (kneeling). PHOTO BY BERTRAND MILES

After the 1976 Olympic
Games, Montreal.
PHOTO BY GREG SLIGHT

Clockwise from top left: Bob Cottingham, Michael Lofton,
me, Csaba, and Steve Mormando.
PHOTO BY BERTRAND MILES

Thanking God on the winner's podium after capturing the individual gold medal in the sabre competition at the 1995 Pan Am Games in Mar del Plata, Argentina.
PHOTO BY CARL BORACK

On the strip at the Atlanta Olympics, 1996.

Some young American fencers in Budapest, Hungary, 1982. Left to right: me, Joe Glucksman, Mike Lofton, Steve Mormando, Stan Leckeach.

At the famous Emperor's Palace during my 1980 trip to China, standing by the statue of the tortoise—a symbol of longevity.

With the U.S. Olympic fencing team in Seoul, 1988.
PHOTO BY CARL BORACK

The U.S. Fencing Team in Italy, 1978. Left to right: John Nonna, Al Davis, Ron Miller, Edgar House, me, Philip Reilly.

Foundation coaches, from left: Aladar Kogler, Don Anthony, me, Eric Rosenberg, Bob Cottingham, Michael Lofton, and Csaba Elthes.
PHOTO BY BERTRAND MILES

Our end-of-the-year awards celebration at the Peter Westbrook Foundation, 1995.
PHOTO BY CARMEN DEJESUS

Supervising a practice bout. PHOTO BY BERTRAND MILES

Eyes on the prize at the PW Foundation.

Posing with Barry Small of the NBA and
Langston Griffin, one of my kids.
PHOTO BY BERTRAND MILES

Presenting an award to Francis
Rodriguez. PHOTO BY BERTRAND MILES

Left to right: Justin Shepard, Julien Miles.
PHOTO BY BERTRAND MILES

Brother and sister future Olympians
Erinn and Keeth Smart.
PHOTO BY TOM SMART

Arthur Ashe (far left) awarding end-of-semester trophies as (left to right) Reverend D. Darrell Griffin, Manhattan Borough President Ruth Messinger, Brian Ledau, Dorian, and Coach Lazarro Mora, Donald Anthony and I (behind Dorian) look on, at the New York Fencers Club, 1993. PHOTO BY BERTRAND MILES

Posing in a classic lunge. PHOTO BY GREG SLIGHT

With Maoris at the Olympic Village in Barcelona, 1992.

Hanging out with a group of Malians at the Olympic Village in Barcelona, 1992.

With Peter Westbrook Foundation kids at the 1996 Olympics in Atlanta. Left to right: Kari Coley, Arin Coley, Steve Mormando, Julien Miles, Aki Spencer-El.

At the 1992 Olympics in Barcelona with (left to right) Aladar Kogler, NBA great David Robinson, and Bob Cottingham.

Carrying the flag at the opening ceremonies of the 1995 Pan Am Games in Argentina. A great honor.

The gold-medal-winning U.S. sabre team at the 1995 Pan Am Games. Left to right: Mike Dasavo, Tomek Strzalkowski, me, John Friedberg.

Celebrating my victory over Gianfranco Dalla Barba of Italy in the 1984 Olympics in Los Angeles. I would then go on to defeat Hervé Granger-Veron for the bronze medal.

With my stepson, Dorian, and Muhammad Ali at the Sports Image Awards in San Francisco, 1995.

Walking down the aisle with Susann under a canopy of swords.
PHOTO BY CARMEN DEJESUS

With Dorian, Vivian, Susann, and Julien Miles, 1992.

My cousin Naohiko as a young boy receiving Noh training from his father.

From left: Vivian, Susann, Dorian, and me.

Wild, Wild West. A gag pose with Bob Cottingham and Don Anthony (left to right, standing), before we captured the sabre team gold medal at the 1989 World Championships in Colorado.

too we are dealing with concentrated human potential. The fighters behind these weapons are very powerful and are trained to deliver many hundreds or even thousands of newtons of force at the tip of their blades. As a result, sometimes things happen that are outside the predictable patterns of the simple laws of mechanics.

One Tuesday afternoon in May, back in 1977, Csaba and I started a routine drill at the New York Fencers Club. Both of us were in top form, and everything we did felt colorful and perfect. Riding high on the effortlessness of our elevated state, we decided to try something unusual and daring. As I ran at him to perform a new move, Csaba thrust his blade out in front of me. I was supposed to deflect it and hit him on the head, but he did it so fast that I actually impaled myself on the tip of his sabre. The blade of a sabre is about two-and-a-half feet long and is very flexible. But as I kept on advancing like a battering ram, I heard it snap about a third of the way from the tip. Realizing that Csaba now had in his hand not a flexible blade with a blunt tip but a rigid knife with a jagged, razor-sharp tip, I threw my head back to avoid his deadly weapon. That move allowed the tip to project below my mask bib and pierce my throat. It went through my larynx and my esophagus, an inch-and-a-half of it. The only witnesses to this near-catastrophe were the unmoving eyes on the portraits of the club's illustrious deceased members.

I felt like there was a big chicken bone or a big fish bone stuck in my throat. The next thing I knew I heard a hissing sound, *pssst pssst*, like when somebody calls to you on the street.

I looked around the room. Who was hissing? What was going on? I suddenly realized that the sound was coming from my own throat. That scared me. When I put my hand over the hole in my throat, the hissing sound stopped. As soon as I removed my hand, the hissing continued. As it turned out, the point had landed precisely in the spot where doctors open up the throat when they perform a tracheotomy. Later, doctors told me that I was the luckiest person in the world. Csaba had done a perfect tracheotomy on me! The neck has so many blood vessels—not to mention the spinal chord—that if the tip had penetrated just a centimeter off, it could have meant death for me. Since the sabre had penetrated the small part of the throat where there are few blood vessels, I had only minimal bleeding.

Normally, Csaba was an arrogant and ornery character; on numerous occasions he was downright nasty. He never showed his softer emotions. He was very tall. His face was a fierce-looking mask—a cross between an owl and an eagle. He had this mean persona. This day proved to be the first and only time I ever saw Csaba break down.

"Ah, Westbrook! Ah, oh no! Westbrook! Westbrook!" Csaba was close to tears as he called to me.

Just witnessing this gave me a kick. The accident had broken through Csaba's rough external facade. In fact, *I* had to console *him*, saying, "Ha! I'm all right." Later I teased him about his reaction.

I decided to wait a couple of minutes to see if I was going to pass out. After about five minutes, my condition seemed stable, so I went upstairs to the locker room. I'm a neat freak, and I take a lot of pride in cleanliness and personal hygiene, but this time I probably took it too far. I was still sweating from having just taken a lesson from Csaba, so I got undressed and took a shower, all the while moving very carefully—three inches at a time. By now fifteen minutes had passed, and I still hadn't passed out.

I convinced Csaba that I was okay, so he left me to my own devices. Being strictly from the school of hard knocks and being a firm believer in living within my means, I took the subway to 14th Street and then walked a couple of blocks to St. Vincent's Hospital. All the way I worried about every bump, knowing that a sudden jolt might make me hemorrhage.

As soon as I entered the emergency ward and showed them what had happened, the doctors rushed me past everyone, shouting, "Knife wound to the neck!" They hooked me up to all kinds of machines and started flooding my system with antibiotics and sugar water. Once they moved me into a room, doctors would file in three times a day to show their students an example of a perfect tracheotomy. They would take the tape off my throat to show them the perfectly placed hole. Through it I could breathe with my mouth and nose closed.

The doctors wanted to keep me in the hospital under observation, but after four-and-a-half days, I wanted out. All I could think about was, *How am I going to train for the Nationals in June?* I was the number one sabrist in the country at the time, and I desperately wanted to hold on to that title. In those days I felt that if I wasn't a champion, I was nothing at all. I knew that if I didn't compete, I would feel lousy for a whole year. I wasn't about to let this injury hold me back. I befriended a nurse who slipped me a two-week supply of antibiotics, and I was on my way.

The next week, I started training with a special neck brace, and the week after that, I competed in the tournament. I was very, very nervous. Every time someone put their blade up to my neck, I would just freeze. In the end, I wasn't able to hold on to the number one spot, but I still managed to place among the top three in the country that year.

The next time I saw Csaba, I couldn't resist teasing him about his uncharacteristically sympathetic reaction. Mocking his awkwardly formal speaking style, I said, "Mr. Sir, I got great joy out of watching you, the Great Csaba, break down like a little child."

He said, "I thought I had killed you—I actually thought I had killed you. When it went in your throat and I pulled it out, I thought I had killed you for sure."

I said, "Yeah, for a minute there, I also thought that maybe I wouldn't make it. Isn't that something?"

At the 1982 World Championships in Rome, the German foilist Matthias Behr was up against the Russian world champion Volodymyr Smirnov and the same sequence of moves had occurred. When Behr riposted, the tip of his foil hit Smirnov's mask and broke off as the Russian advanced. The broken tip had pierced the mask. Smirnov took three steps, stopped, fell in a heap, went into small convulsions, and then became inert. The doctors on the scene declared him basically dead except for some faint brain stem activity. They put him on a respirator while the tournament continued, as the Russians realized that it was too late to revive him. When they got him to the hospital, they took him off the respirator: Smirnov was dead. They found that the foil had penetrated above his eyebrow and through his skull to a depth of seven inches. Such is the awesome force behind the blade. This was the tragic event that resulted in stronger masks being mandated.

When the tip of the blade breaks off, its trajectory can be totally unpredictable. In 1994 when I was practicing at the club, an inch of my tip broke off and the missile somehow landed on my calf muscle. Dark blood started pouring out and the pain was vicious. At the hospital, they sewed me up and gave me a tetanus shot and I recovered fully. Accidents do happen, no matter how many precautions we take. Very rarely, however, have I seen serious accidents happen in practice or during casual light fencing. Usually the big accidents happen at world tournaments with high-level performers, where they are relying on their killer instinct to compete at their very best. These fencers have more than their own expectations to meet. They are fighting to win for their teammates, their families, their country, and the whole world, and they really don't want to let all those people down. In that arena, with the spotlight on them, they are driven to find the Superman in themselves. Unlike in running, where you are running for yourself, or in basketball, where you have to be a good team player, in fencing you're in one-on-one combat, using everything you have to destroy your opponent. Some of the contestants from poor Eastern European countries have a lot on the line. Losing can mean not having the money to support your family. The stress can be explosive.

One time I saw an Eastern European fencer get so worked up trying to make the World Championships that right after the last touch, his emotional system completely shut down. He fainted, collapsed, and banged his head on the ground. Two minutes later he recovered. I was standing close to him.

"Did I win? Did I win?" These were his first words.

"Did you win? Yeah, you won," I told him. But what I was really thinking was, *Shouldn't you be wondering how you ended up on the ground and whether you're hurt?* He was emotionally overloaded and his system had crashed for a few minutes, but now he was happy. This was not the first time it had happened to him. He had a problem that could get worse. I don't think anyone in that situation should be allowed to continue to fence. What if he hadn't regained consciousness?

Fencing has trained me to defeat my opponent. I use all my power and anger and everything else I have against him. All my life I have practiced unleashing my power against my enemy. The concentrated fury that one learns to unleash is not something that can be easily turned on and off. After winning my Olympic medal, I realized that I was still a very angry individual, a real-life raging bull. When you're in training for a top competition like the Olympics, anger can sometimes be helpful. It can give you a kind of fuel to help you achieve your goal. But once the competition is over, you don't need it any more. In fact, it can start to wear you down.

After the '84 Olympics, I still felt an incredible rage in me, like I was ready to erupt. I'd been running after the

Olympic dream for so many years that I didn't know what to do with myself once I achieved it. I assumed the medal would erase all my problems and bring me instant happiness, peace, and joy. Needless to say, it didn't. That left me angry and frustrated. I realized something was very wrong, and I knew that with my anger raging out of control, I'd never be able to figure out what it was.

The ability to switch your power on or off at will can be learned. This is not an easy thing to do, yet in many ways, it is the most important thing for an athlete to learn. If you are a professional boxer and somebody confronts you in the street, it is going to be damn hard to keep from reacting like you would in the ring unless you've trained yourself to do so. Somebody steps on your toe and you are ready to kill them. This is a dangerous situation. Lack of control has led to the defeat of many a competitor outside the sports arena.

I think that in my forties, I have finally trained myself to control my aggression. I used to keep my anger in a tightly shut jar. A lot of pressure could build up in that jar, and I never knew when the lid would pop, the glass would shatter, and the whole thing would explode. Now, after years of focusing my awareness on the actual movements of my thoughts and energy, I find that my anger is in an *open jar*. I still have it contained, I can still take it with me, but it's no longer locked in like hot steam in a pressure cooker. I have more control because I know it won't explode. This is my condition, and it has its uses.

Living in New York has given me plenty of chances to test my own stability during "close shaves" in the city's streets and subways. In the subway, where people get insanely territorial, I saw a guy literally stomp and kick a mentally disturbed homeless man to death for spitting at his child. It was an excessive reaction, and horrible to see. No one, including myself, intervened. I could have stopped the guy if I had let myself. But I knew that if he had a gun he probably would have shot anyone who dared to intervene. I chose, on this occasion, not to risk my life. Later it was reported in the papers that the courts let the guy off. Does this mean that our society condones deadly violence, or that it doesn't value the lives of some of its citizens?

Another time, I was riding the A train and out of the blue, a man started swinging on the pole overhead and smashing out the windows with his heavy combat boots. People were screaming and backing away. Because of my conditioning, I didn't even get up. This lunatic was about three feet away from me, and I was calmly watching his antics. When he looked at me, I looked straight back at him and said, "Stay right there. Don't even look in my direction. Keep doing what you're doing, that's your business." Of course, I was prepared to destroy him if he approached me. Should I feel remorse for my decision? Should I have moved away and started to pray instead of thinking, *If he comes over here, I'm going to bust his ass?*

On the street one time I stepped on someone's heel by mistake. Immediately I said loudly, "I'm sorry." I had on a suit and tie.

"I should punch you in your face," the man said as he rushed up to me. Since my reflexes are extremely fast, I let him get right up to my face. He even lifted his hand. I stood my ground till the very last moment, waiting to see if he had the audacity to carry out his threat. I gave him a look that said, _If you actually swing that arm, I'll have to go to war with my suit on in the middle of the street._

"Heh, heh, heh, I was just playing," he said, sensing danger.

"I know _damn well_ you were playing."

"I didn't mean anything, brother." He was trying to get out of it.

"No problem, brother." We shook hands and he walked away.

I'm not used to backing down when challenged, and sometimes my fighting instincts still get the better of me. One day I was riding the subway with my good friend and fencing buddy Don Anthony. A big dude seated across from us looked at me and said, "What the fuck are you looking at?"

"You," I said.

"If you say one more word to me, I'm going to kick your fucking ass in the subway."

Everyone was listening and some people were backing away. Don seemed concerned.

"I can think of a lot of words. Which one don't you want me to say?" I replied calmly.

He stood up and said, "Brother, I will fuck you up if you come over here right on this train in front of all these people. Do you understand me?"

I walked over to him, gently and put my arm around his

shoulder, looked into his eyes, and said, "I'll fuck *you* up. Can you hear me?" Then I realized, *Damn, people are looking at me. Let me relax myself.*

I took my arm off his back but tapped him on the shoulder.

"You got a dollar you can spare?" he asked me shamelessly as he sidled away.

The point I am trying to make here is that even my "open jar" policy is not appropriate on all occasions. In this case, I should have just said sorry and walked away no matter what. I'm still so ready to meet negative challenges that I'm afraid some day I could get hurt or lose my life for being that way. I could have chosen not to make that warlike show of strength. Instead, I was checking somebody else's wayward behavior. Could it be all that Zorro and Superman I had watched on TV? Deep down I know I can't always win in confrontations. When I take up a challenge and make the other guy back down, I win. But I know that this kind of victory does not make me more of a man. In fact I feel like *less* of a man for acting out my warlike qualities.

Lately, in the comfort and safety of my apartment, I have started visualizing various hazardous situations. I invoke God and my ancestors, and then I watch myself play out the situation as if I were in a movie. For instance, say I encounter some crazy person like the one Don and I met on the subway and we start talking, and suddenly he says to me, "Shut the fuck up! Don't say another word!" Well, in my mind I run through my options. I could back down and not say another word, but that's not my nature. I could let there be a confrontation, but that's no longer the way I like to operate. So now what do I do? I say to myself, *Let me put my ego aside. Let me not get into fencing in life.* I actually think to myself, *Here I am, on the line again. Shall I stay in the safety zone, or shall I step into the danger zone like I always do? No, this time I am going to stay over here.* I enact this scenario in my mind as clearly as possible. I play back the negative experiences I've had, and plug in a different chip to get a positive result. I consciously decide what I want the outcome of the situation to be. To avert personal harm, I create a happy and positive ending as opposed to a negative one. This is part of my survival training.

One of my favorite pastimes is working out at a karate dojo. A lot of guys in these urban dojos are gunslingers. Pure, raw gunslingers. Gangsters. When I started out, I was a white belt, a beginner, and they look upon white belts like they're dirt. But within a few days, the guys picked up on my training and came to me, asking, "Can we be with you? Would you like to hang out and train with us?" I welcomed the suggestion. I had earned my rank.

Everything goes back to openness and training. If you choose to remain a knucklehead, that's your problem. You won't pick up the skills you're looking for even if you work at it for eighty years. But if you're sensitive and intelligent, you can cut down the learning process and find the shortest route to where you want to go. As I see it, if we let our sensitivity and softness get calloused like the hard hands of a karate practitioner, we are missing the whole point. Some Eastern teachings state that the true test of a grandmaster of a lethal martial artform is when children and animals can relax in their company. So in some respects, the better we get at the form, the more sensitive we should be to the human condition. That is my ideal. Blind indifference in the face of life-threatening danger is not bravery. It is a form of depravity, a dehumanization of the human condition, an attitude I hope never to have.

Here is a vivid example of a state to avoid. In the subway, a middle-aged man sitting next to me lights up a cigarette and starts puffing on it as though he's in his own private smoking room.

"Can you put that cigarette out please?" says a man sitting directly across from this smokestack by my side. I am observing the interaction closely. One never knows these days how people are going to behave.

"No, it's a free country," he responds, and keeps on smoking. I can see people shifting uneasily in their seats.

Then the man across the aisle stands up and pulls out a knife. "There's no smoking on a subway. Can you put that cigarette out?!" he says firmly, and without waiting for another response, he casually steps across the aisle and stabs and slashes the smoker four times in his chest. Amazingly, the man next to me doesn't even resist or cry out. He just sits there smoking. Again, like in an old cop show, people scatter out of the way, screaming, but I stay in my seat, looking at both of them very calmly.

Before the assailant gets off at the next station, he turns to the smoker again and says, "I thought I told you to put the cigarette out."

"It is *still* a free country," the smoker replies, and keeps on dragging on the butt of his cigarette. The guy with the knife steps off, shaking his head in total disbelief.

Finally, I can no longer contain myself. "My man, why don't you shut up?" I ask the smoker to his face. "Are you crazy?"

I don't mind risking my life for somebody in trouble, but not *this* nut who clearly had his values all mixed up. My own calmness under the circumstances again surprised me. I guess it's my survival tool, keeping me alive, knowing which things aren't worth fighting for.

COMING BACK FOR GOLD 7

"**P**eter, why don't you try to make the Pan American Games?" There was Csaba, on my case again.

In the fall of 1994 I was forty-two years old. I had been semi-retired from competitive tournaments since Barcelona, and wasn't planning to go to any more international games. My body was not what it used to be and my foundation was taking up more and more of my time. I was resigned to the notion that it was time to pass on the baton. After five Pan Am and five Olympic games, I no longer felt the need to prove myself in fencing. I had a whole trunkload of medals and trophies in storage. Moreover, I had been skipping try-outs lately. I didn't even want to try out because I knew what it would take. It would take too much of my time, energy, perseverance, and sweat.

But Csaba wouldn't give up. "Do you realize that you don't have any motivation? You're becoming lazy. You don't have any initiative. What's the matter with you? You can do it *easily.*"

I didn't think I could do it easily. And at forty-two, I didn't care. Why should I, when the average retirement age for competitive fencing is about thirty-four.

He said, "Peter, come on. You can do this. Don't get soft. If you can do this at forty-two, do you know what an upset that would be? You would make history. Just to be able to do something that nobody else has done would say a lot about you. It would make the whole world wonder how this could be happening in a sport where most of the athletes are much younger, often in their teens and in their twenties. No one would believe it. Sir, I give you good advice. Just come in twice a week, and with no effort, you'll make the Pan Am games."

Csaba went on and on. He seemed to have no doubt regarding my ability. After a whole lot of taunting and plenty of pep talks, he had me nailed.

I decided to give it a shot.

Anyone in the country who can afford it can try out for the Pan American Games. There are five separate national tournaments, all open to the public. In each tournament, you win a certain number of points depending on how you place: first place is worth 1,000 points, second place 800, third place 700, fifth place 400—all the way down to twentieth place. At the end of the season, the four fencers who have accumulated the most points out of the hundreds of people who participate get to be on the American team. Of these four fencers, the top two compete in the individual matches, the top three play on the team, and the fourth fencer is used as an alternate.

I started training with Csaba like we used to. I also took up weight training with Gary Guerriero, a physical therapist and trainer for the New York Islanders. Working with Gary helped me to regain some of the muscle I had lost over the years. I took part in three tryouts, and placed high in all three. In fact, I had accumulated enough points to make me the top American contender for the Pan American Games. I found this hard to believe. Maybe it was destiny for me to come back for another Pan American gold.

Despite my numbers, though, the United States Fencing Association discouraged my participation in the games. The message they sent me was that I no longer had it and I simply couldn't win. Their position was that tryouts at home were one thing, but at the Pan American Games, with top contenders from North America, South America, Central America, and Cuba, I would be up against formidable opposition. They felt that fencing world class and with much younger fencers would be an entirely different ballgame. They suggested I let someone younger go even if they weren't quite as good as me, because for them the experience would be an essential training ground for future competitions.

The USFA officials and numerous coaches conceded that my experience and skills were exceptional, but stressed that I would still be up against people in their twenties. I would be unfamiliar with their style, my legs would not be as agile, and therefore they would easily beat me. Fencing is a young man's game, and the game had changed in the last three or four years. Fleching, for example, which is a running attack, was no longer allowed. Without the advantage of speed that fleching gives you, it is harder to score. Since I hadn't competed with these new fencers, I didn't have a good sense of how to beat them. And with this undoubtedly being my last international tournament, the inevitable result would be a loss to both me and the USFA.

Their observations were certainly valid. I thought a lot about them and discussed the issues with my coach. Even though the odds were not in my favor, Csaba persisted, saying, "It is possible that you may not be successful, but I believe you will be successful and you do too. The main reason why everyone thinks that it's impossible is because it's just not done! No one competes at the age of forty-two! If you win, it will send a shock wave all over the fencing world. It will be a shock to the Olympic committee. It will make everybody think. You should go to the Pan American Games, and the '96 Olympics, too!"

Finally I made my decision. I decided to treat the USFA's words of caution as a challenge. My competitive spirit told me that it was better to fight than to subject myself to psychological retirement. In my heart of hearts I felt that regardless of what others thought, I had to remember that I had a special talent that, by its very nature, had the capacity to outdo itself. All that was needed was the right opportunity.

When we arrived in Mar del Plata, Argentina, the site of the 1995 Pan Am Games, our hosts bused the entire U. S. team, 700 American athletes, to a village they had constructed especially for us. Mar del Plata is a summer resort town on the Atlantic whose residents proved to be wonderfully relaxed, unlike the big city folks up north in Buenos Aires. Having been to Argentina before, I knew that Argentineans love Americans. Between the warm reception, the beautiful people, the beaches, and the hot tango nightclubs, we all felt happy to be there.

As if the high I was experiencing from making a comeback wasn't enough, the U. S. team voted to have me carry the flag at the opening ceremony. That was an honor I never expected, especially since I had already carried Old Glory at the '92 Olympics in Barcelona. It was incredible to be picked from among so many world-class American athletes. So once again, I carried the flag proudly for our country.

To this day I don't know what I'm more proud of: to have carried the flag for the USA or to have been the bearer of the flag as an African American. Emotionally I was celebrating my victory as a triumph for my people. Often having to prove ourselves in the eyes of whites, this was already a win for blacks and generally for people of color. That is just the kind of crazy world we live in. I was only the second African-American male to carry the flag for a U. S. Olympic team. Decathlete Rafer Johnson was flag-bearer at the 1960 Rome games. Track-and-field champion Evelyn Ashford became the first African-American woman to have this honor when carried the flag during the opening ceremonies of the 1988 Olympics in Seoul, South Korea.

I was able to see up close the mixed reaction my selection caused within the international athletic community. Obviously the people who voted for me were happy. Also, plenty of white people seemed proud that I was selected for this honor. But it wasn't easy for everyone to accept the sight of a black man carrying the flag in the opening ceremony— the first one up representing America. I could almost hear their thoughts: *He's carrying the flag because of his seniority. Bet he won't do anything else. He's been around so long—that's the only reason why they voted him in.* Some people even joked around, saying, "Why don't you let someone else hold the flag? Aren't your arms getting tired?" I made it clear to them that I could hold that flag for days without getting tired.

One white reporter from a newspaper out of Passaic, New Jersey, came up to me and said, "Boy, they got any old body carrying the flag these days, don't they? All you have to do is hang around long enough and you'll get to carry the flag."

I thought to myself: *My God! What a nasty, negative thing to say!* All I could say to him was, "That's not true, Sir."

"Sure it is," he said.

I kept my cool and continued. "Sir, there are a lot of people who have been in the Pan American Games just as long as I have. There are people in the equestrian sports and people in shooting who are in their fifties. People much older than me could have carried the flag, but they didn't. I didn't qualify because of my age or my longevity in my sport. The people elected me, so what you're saying is not true." He finally walked away, but another reporter with a similar attitude took his place. I was really hurt by them, but I kept up the attitude: *That's life. Lemme keep moving on.*

All my early euphoria evaporated when I encountered the man who had been my nemesis at the last Pan American

Games and one of the U. S. team's most formidable adversaries. At the end of the first day of the tournament, I noticed that every member of the Cuban fencing team was staring at me. They knew who I was because they knew my history. Only the top two fencers from each country compete in the individual matches, and since the other top American had just been eliminated, they realized their champion would be up against me. They must have been thinking, *Westbrook? That old guy? Damn!* They knew I was forty-two years old, and they knew that at the last Pan American Games four years before I had only competed in the team slot. I hadn't qualified to compete in an individual position. They must have assumed I was history. Yet here I was, back after four years, about to fence their number one guy. It just didn't make sense!

The Cubans approached me and we exchanged greetings. Now I recognized one of them: a very dark-skinned and fierce-looking man in his twenties. His name was Aristedes Faure, but everyone called him Fabio. At the last Pan American Games he had decimated me and everybody else on our team to win the gold medal in sabre fencing. Fabio walked up to me, bringing his six-foot four-inch frame within twelve inches of my face. I am just over five-foot nine. He stared down at me, his face distorted in a nasty sneer. He seemed to be looking down on *everything*. At first I thought this was a practical joke because he looked like he wanted to tear me to pieces.

"Wehbroo," he finally uttered, "I'm going to fuck you!"

I couldn't believe my ears. We were not fencing and we didn't have any sabres in our hands and it wasn't like we were specifically talking about fencing. So I said, "I beg your pardon?"

Fabio moved a little closer. At this point he was about six inches from me. That's kind of close to be saying *that* to someone. I hadn't seen him in four years and he was not my friend. To me his face was conveying the message, *I am black, I am Cuban, and I am strong.* It was scary. He inched even closer but I didn't budge.

He spoke again, repeating the earlier threat, and adding the word "man" at the end.

I thought to myself, *Oh my God.* I looked up hard to see if there was the hint of a smile hidden somewhere in his grimace. Finding none, all I could say was, "Come on, let's do it right now." I think he got my drift. His teammates pulled him away a little bit just to calm him down. When I ran into him again later in the day, he looked at me with a knowing sneer.

For the next three days, Fabio's threats turned out to be far more than a typical combative boast. On the practice strip he went through every member of the U. S. sabre team, myself included, like a hot knife through butter. Even when I was putting out 110 percent and doing my darnedest to make him think that I wasn't afraid, I knew he was clearly a superior fencer and that I was in deep trouble. The whole world would be watching us.

Fabio fenced twice a day every day, including Sundays— long, drawn out sessions that ran from 9:00 to 12:00 in the morning and from 2:00 to 4:30 in the afternoon. He'd been keeping up this routine for years. Now it added up to make him four years stronger than me at approximately half my age! I knew this guy was a serious professional, and he knew the

odds were in his favor. All my teammates seemed to be prepared for the worst. I thought differently. Strange as it may
sound, I still believed I could win.

The night before the match, in the privacy of my room,
I got down on my knees and invoked the Creator, all the
forces of nature, and all of my ancestors. I urgently appealed
with unwavering concentration and humility: _I did not come
here out of pride and stubbornness. You helped me to come here
against all odds and against the advice of everybody except my
teacher. Now please guide me and help me show the world that I
didn't come here in vain. Grant me your protection and show me
the power of Your activity. Let me be Your vehicle. You have never
lost a battle and You have never ignored a sincere appeal for help.
You have brought me this far—please help me finish this job. If
You help me win, I will kneel down before everybody to let them
know that I won only because of You._

Right before we fenced for the gold medal, the Cuban
stared down at me and muttered, "Hmm—now you're finally
going to get what I've been promising you for the last three
days." From the corner of my eye I glimpsed another Cuban
champion slice his finger across his throat to indicate that I
would indeed be beheaded on that fateful day.

Everything I'd been training for came down to this one
match. The pressure was on. It didn't help to hear a few people still saying to me, "Westbrook, what are you doing here?
Who are you coaching?" But by then I was on automatic pilot.

When the match began, I felt scared and nervous inside,
but since the Cuban had an incredible air of confidence, I put
on the same air. I said my prayers. I prayed for the spirit to

turn my sabre into a magic wand so I'd be able to teach him a lesson and perform some magic right there in front of everybody. I prayed for the Zone to hit me in my moment of need.

The first point went to me. He attacked. I made a block—they call it a parry—and a riposte. I got the second touch, too, but he was coming on strong. Next thing I know, it's 5-0, but I know it's still a long way to get to fifteen touches. Here he gets a point on me. Now I start attacking him. I can see and smell the fear in him. I see it in his face. I see what I've been training all my life to see: fear. I see it in his body language. I see it in his emotions. I see nothing but fear. I get 6, 7, and 8. Now I realize that when I see this type of fear, I have to jump on him hard, because if I don't, he may rise up again. Like they say, "The South is gonna rise up again!" So I stomp on him. I let him feel my power, I let him feel my emotions, I let him feel my arrogance. I even verbalize and say a few words and let him feel them. I let everybody in the whole audience feel my power. I let the officials feel my power. By then I know that the magic has been granted to me: I am in the Zone. Now I even get his own self against him. I pounce on him and I beat him and beat him.

Once it was around 12-3, I knew he couldn't win. Now it was my turn to laugh. I could score on him so easily that I could do whatever I wished. I even let him get a couple more points. Then I started acting like a matador with a bull, flaunting and making games and putting on a little showmanship. I started to make a monkey out of him. In my mind's eye, I could see him being whittled down inch by inch from his six-foot four frame.

Professional fencing matches tend to run very close. Average contest scores are usually 15-14, 15-13, 15-12, and so on. For example, 15-11 is considered an excellent score for the winner. I beat this Cuban 15 to 5! Even when I was nineteen years old I couldn't have beaten him 15 to 5! People were astonished. They all stood up with their mouths gaping.

I was overcome with such emotion that standing with my teammates on the raised stage, in front of hundreds of people, I bowed down three times on my knees, looked up in the air, and said, "Thanks." When I won my bronze medal at the 1984 Olympic Games in Los Angeles, and when I won the gold medal at the 1983 Pan American Games, I did not get down on my knees. In the past I would have been embarrassed and felt awkward, thinking people might laugh at me. But this time I didn't care about what people would think of me. I *had* to give thanks where thanks were due. When I got up for the third time, everyone ran onto the stage and threw me up in the air. "Hooray, you won! Hooray, you won!"

Meanwhile, for Fabio to have been defeated 15-5 in front of the Cuban nation and in front of all the Latinos who were rooting for him was a terrible humiliation. I had embarrassed him and I could see that. He looked like he was ready to cry. But after the match he actually gave me a hug, and from that day on he showered me with admiration and respect. He had been humbled. I could see the difference in his face. He would smile as he said, "I can't believe you actually did that!"

The Pan American Games attract contestants from most parts of the Western hemisphere—North America, South America, Central America, and Cuba—as well as spectators from Europe. All the top European fencers in the audience came up to me to greet me. Olympic gold medalists from Hungary said, "Westbrook, *Grõtõ Lãluk!*" which is "Congratulations" in Hungarian. Even the Cuban champion who had suggested before the match that I was going to be beheaded came up to me and bowed low. He told me he had never seen anything like my performance.

At the end of the games, some of those same unhappy reporters who expressed their cynicism when I carried the flag at the opening ceremonies were dumbstruck. "How did you do it?" they asked.

The most interesting moment, however, was probably when an official from the USFA came up to me and said, "Wow! We knew you could do it!" I couldn't help thinking to myself, *You must have a very unusual way of expressing your confidence, because that's not what you said before.*

I said to him, "I beg your pardon? *I* knew I could do it, and my coach knew, but nobody else knew because it hadn't been done before." And given the odds, how could anybody be expected to think any differently?

Back in the U. S. a week later, when I first entered the modest precinct of the New York Fencers Club, my home base, I finally understood what Csaba had been trying to tell me before I left. Everybody without exception—coaches and players, adults and children—stopped what they were doing. Clashing swords fell silent, masks came off, and I received a standing ovation.

Csaba died of a massive stroke in Budapest in the fall of 1995, and was buried there among his countrymen—a European to the end. A memorial service was scheduled to take place in New York during the second week of December at the Hungarian Catholic Church on East 86th Street. Half an hour before the service was to begin, Csaba's dear friend Mr. Chaba Pallaghy, a fellow Hungarian fencer who had also come to America in 1956, called me at the Fencers Club where I was getting ready to go to the ceremony. Unfortunately, because of a record-breaking snowstorm that day, Mr. Pallaghy would not be able to attend. He asked me if I would help deliver the eulogy in his place. I would have been comfortable just sitting with the congregation and listening to what people had to say. I'd been with Csaba over half my life, so to me it wasn't a time to speak, but to listen and think and reflect. Nevertheless, duty called, so I managed to improvise a speech.

I said that Csaba was a great man who was different from other people. Everyone has their own way of giving. Just as surgeons give through their knowledge of anatomy and surgical techniques, Csaba gave through fencing. If you asked Csaba for something that was not related to fencing, he would respond through fencing. On countless occasions he gave poor but promising students free fencing lessons. Not too many doctors, lawyers, or corporate executives are going to give you free check-ups, legal advice, or business tips. He was a very, very giving person when it came to the sport of fencing. I acknowledged that I owed him a whole lot for who I was and what I had accomplished.

"Peter, I made you," Csaba once told me.

And I replied, "Sir, you didn't make me. God used you to help me, and he used me to help you."

"You're right," Csaba agreed. I never knew him to say "you're right" about anything before then or since.

Csaba taught me about fencing, but indirectly he taught me about life. He tried to pour into me all that he knew. Now that I think about it, Csaba and my mother were very similar. They were both strict disciplinarians who didn't show a lot of warmth—though you could see the warmth behind everything they did. Csaba would give me advice about everything: how to deal with women, when to get married, how to handle my career, the etiquette of dealing with white people and with other fencers. I spent more time with this man than I did with my father and mother combined. And he never let me forget that I had "wasted" a whole year in college when I stopped training with him. "If you had stayed with me then, Peter, you would have *more* national titles, *more* Pan American medals, *more* World Championship finals, *more* Olympic experience."

Csaba Elthes was passionate about the future of fencing in the United States, and believed the sport offered great hope for African Americans. After I started my foundation, he loved to spend time watching the young fencers. He always pointed out to me the ones he thought had that special talent. "Black people are the future of this sport," Csaba would say. "If we had some of those same professionals from baseball and basketball, Peter, just think of where fencing would be today!"

With his technical skills and God's grace, Csaba guided me to five Olympic games in a row. He died too soon to see me at my sixth Olympics in Atlanta, but since he was the one who urged me to compete there, he was very much with me in spirit. It was his biggest dream and wish for me.

"Peter, go for six Olympic games."

"Are you crazy? I've had enough. Five Olympic games—that's twenty years. I'm satisfied."

"Please, Peter, you've *got* to do it. For yourself. For me."

At Atlanta and beyond, my efforts are dedicated to the memory of Csaba and my mother and their wishes for me.

ZONING IN ATLANTA

8

My sixth and last Olympic Games was a bittersweet experience. Once again, it was a special privilege and honor to be part of the great international gathering of top athletes and strong-willed individuals known as the Olympics. I have always found it exhilarating to be with people of different colors, sexes, languages, sizes, shapes, eyes, religions, and different social and economic backgrounds—to all be together to compete with one another in the spirit of friendship. Every time I go to an Olympics, I feel like I am witnessing the glory of God to see people, whose nations might be hard at war, bonding as comrades and fellow humans. At the Olympic Village it is quite common to see two athletes hug each other and cry on each others' shoulders recognizing the beauty of humanity in each other.

On the flip side, the Games can also be a hotbed of personal and political hostility. In my case, I felt the sting of agism when I saw that some of my fellow athletes thought it was high time for me to pass the baton. More generally, the stakes are so high in these competitions that many people lose their calm and succumb to hysteria. And as history has sadly but perhaps meaningfully shown, competitors and spectators alike have used the Olympic Games as a place to stage their grievances for all the world to see.

So it was in Atlanta, when a deafening bomb exploded right next door to the building I was in. A shower of glass from a huge plate-glass window rained down on my wife, my sister-in-law, and me as we lay face down on the ground. That was scary stuff, but it was over as suddenly as it occurred. None of us got hurt. Luckily, security personnel had already evacuated most of the crowd from the vicinity of the unaccompanied bag. As we were whisked away from the scene by bus, our eyes fell on the bloodshed, loss of life, and mayhem that some madman had caused.

Qualifying for Atlanta '96 was a sweet victory for me. Naturally, conditions were not in my favor to make it this time. I was forty-four years old, competing against people in their early twenties. I was old enough to be their daddy, and some of them were even calling me "Granddaddy." Yet I became one of the five fencers on the men's sabre team with relative ease, considering what most of the contestants had to go through to qualify. The Olympics have never been the exclusive province of the young. In fact, part of the beauty of this great event is that eligibility is determined strictly by one's performance. Many contestants who want to make the team accumulate expensive points in the foreign arena, while I hedged my bets by fencing mostly at tournaments in the United States. As luck would have it, that was enough.

The Olympics is a great leveler of hopes and expectations. I was in line to compete against Lurane Williams, a young black fencer from England. Williams was the sole black fencer on the British team. We had competed against each other in tournaments a couple of times before. I knew him to be a strong but sweet guy with a military background who was a talented martial artist as well as a strong fencer. He told me he had trained with coaches who had closely studied my style of fencing. Apparently, I'd been a role model for him throughout his fencing career.

Before our match, I wanted to play a few psychological games with him. A lot of athletes use these kind of mind games to get an extra edge. So I went up to him, looked him in the face, and tried to put my arms around him and give him a big hug. He didn't want to do that. The next time I saw him, I went up to him and said, "How you doin'?" and tried to shake his hand. He didn't want to do that either. Later on, we were standing together waiting to get our equipment checked. I was two inches from him and his hand was on the table. I moved his hand and put mine where his was, as if to say, "Go away from me, boy." I tried to rattle him as I always try to rattle people before my event because I know that if I beat him psychologically, he'll already be at a disadvantage.

When it came time for our bout, I felt utterly confident. Williams got the first touch and I got the second touch. Then he got the next two touches. All of a sudden I realized, *I'm not so confident anymore.* But I summoned back my confidence because I knew that was what I needed. Then he got a couple more touches. Now my confidence was gone. My insecurity returned. I knew from experience that I had to get my feeling back, I had to get rid of the tightness. I tried as best as I could, but he kept the pressure on me. He wasn't as young emotionally as I'd taken him to be. In fact, he was very strong-willed. I became aware that the American public was watching me fall behind, and that increased the pressure. Usually I could pull myself out of this, but the match went on and I felt myself sinking lower and lower and lower until it was over.

I knew I was a better fencer than this guy, and yet he beat me badly, 15-8. I was devastated in my first match. Was he more favored than I? Talk about harnessing anger! I had to practice what I preach about stepping back and looking at the whole picture to get a handle on what is going on. A lot of anger surfaced within me. I felt very frustrated. Simply knowing that my reflexes were faster, my experience deeper, my rhythm and technique more perfected than the other guy's didn't help me in that match. Even though I had prayed every day for I don't know how long, at the end of it all, I had to face the fact that this kid had defeated me by a wide margin. It was a crushing loss and a painful experience. I stepped off the strip feeling stunned.

Then the strangest thing happened. A flock of reporters started swarming around me instead of Williams. I, the loser, was getting all the attention. I had not prepared for this but this time I had enough wits about me to realize that I had to step back and try to see the whole picture. When I did, I saw that my anger was not real. I realized that I shouldn't be dwelling on what happened during those fateful three minutes on the strip: *I lost in front of everybody. So many people were counting on me to win. I must look like an idiot.* Many such thoughts crowded my head. Only when I took a deep breath and made an effort not to be swept off my feet by such emotions could I stay calm enough to actually hear the questions they were throwing at me and to answer them in a coherent fashion. As it turned out, there were four reporters armed with cameras and notebooks and I was able to talk calmly about what had happened and what I was going through.

I now realize that I was a bit too tight during my match with Williams. I wanted that win too much to be relaxed. The winning state is sort of like an elusive butterfly in your hand. If you hold the creature too tightly you squeeze it to death, and if you're too slack you let it fly away. I wanted so much to go out with a glorious bang that I forgot the most important thing: to be flexible. I couldn't even do my everyday type of fencing, which is generally loose and relaxed. Although I was able to keep my wits about me after that defeat, it hurt like crazy. *Why do I have to get this lesson now?* I wondered. It still hurts.

A few days later, the press came to me for more stories. I became the most media-covered fencer in the country and possibly the world. Bryant Gumbel, Jim Lampley, and Dick Enberg each did an extended interview with me and the interviews aired on prime time. I spoke about how fencing in America has become an urban grassroots phenomenon. They were all very kind to me, and I only hope that all the positive feedback I received means that I'll be able to help more kids in the future. But in general, press and TV coverage of our sport was terrible at the '96 Olympics, and I felt bad for my colleagues who didn't get the attention that they deserved. The simultaneous video playback of the fencing matches that the audience saw on two huge screens at the games was spectacular. But it has still not convinced major sponsors that fencing is an exciting sport that will capture the popular American imagination if given a chance. That day will come.

Luckily for me I had a second chance in Atlanta to prove to myself and to others that I had not lost my touch. I had one more match left—the sabre team event—and I had only two days to overcome the devastation of losing to Williams before returning to the strip. The only thing I had to get me going again was my spiritual outlook. To turn a bad situation into an advantage, I asked myself, *What can I learn from this? What is the spiritual value of me coming here, training, dedicating this tournament to Csaba and my mother, listening to negative remarks from people who feel that I shouldn't even be here, and then getting beat like a dog in front of everybody? What is the benefit of this to me? I see no value in it.* All of this came into my mind in a couple of seconds. Then I saw what the benefit was. It was not for me. It was for the foundation. People would see my story and feel the pulse of my organization, the work that we're doing there. I saw that going to my sixth and last Olympic Games would ultimately mean more recognition and funding for my foundation.

In a team match, there are three players on each side competing in a total of nine five-point bouts. The players are rotated after each bout, and the first team to make forty-five touches wins. In our match with the Canadians, the situation was already bad for us by the time I took my final rotation on the strip. It was the ninth bout—our last chance in this match. According to the rules, the final bout is played out to the end until one side reaches forty-five touches. The Canadian team had forty touches. We were behind with thirty-two. Their player only needed five points to win; I needed thirteen. The loss would be a bad one for the U. S. sabre team, since it was our last match and it would determine whether we placed ninth or tenth. It was also my last Olympic hurrah.

When I stepped onto the strip, it was 99 percent certain that the Canadian team would win. I was up against Jean-Paul Banos, one of Canada's best fencers, the same guy who had beat me at the 1987 Pan American Games. I said to myself, _Let me see if I can let go of all that anxiety that constricted me two days ago._ As the match began, I was able to let it go. I found that I got the first few touches easily. Then I realized that something even greater was going on. I said to myself, _Oh my God, the gift is in my hand._ Miraculously, the Zone had descended. It landed on me and worked just like spinach works on Popeye. I didn't know how long the gift would last, but after three touches, I could feel it more and more. Because of my experience, I was able to keep running with this Zoning, this spiritual gift. The result was that I scored thirteen touches in a row and won the bout. My opponent was only able to score three.

This sort of pattern is almost unheard of, if not impossible, but it happened. I had overcome insurmountable odds.

I instantly relearned what I had forgotten and turned what was going to be a bad defeat into a golden opportunity. Throughout my fencing career I had upset people by winning when it was least expected. Losing the individual match had prepared me to help bring our team to victory. It had been a necessary emotional and psychological sacrifice.

I was as spellbound by the magic as my teammates were. The audience was equally spellbound, because the unbelievable was happening, just like in a cartoon. They never saw fencing like that before, and they were shouting, whistling, and whooping it up in response. My teammates were so ecstatic that they threw me up in the air three times with everybody watching. I must have been about seven feet up in the air as hundreds of Americans ran down the aisles to say thanks. This was very unusual. We had only finished in ninth place. But had we lost, we wouldn't have placed at all. My new coach, Steve Mormando, was beside himself with joy. Afterwards, when people patiently lined up to talk to us and to get our autographs, it seemed as though everybody was truly inspired by what they had witnessed that day.

One of my friends overheard someone—must have been a Canadian—say, "Face it. It was a lousy team and they just got lucky." Whoever said that was missing the most important thing: To me, you are only lucky if, when the opportunity presents itself, you're able to take advantage of it. Without the dedication and the hard work, you'll never be able to run with it. So basically I have no problems with being lucky. All in all, "lucky" was a beautiful way to end my Olympic career.

PART TWO

BLACK LIKE ME

9

I have always been amazed by the things people will say to me because I'm biracial.

"Man, Pete, it's too bad you're a black guy, but at least you're half-Asian!"

Or another variation on the same theme:

"Pete, y'know, you're not black."

"I'm not?"

"No, you're not black like those niggers. You know what you are? You're Japanese. Look, you *know* you are different. Come hang out with us."

The Asian part of me has always been less threatening or more appealing to certain people. Some have even taken me into their confidence to inquire, "Pete, have you noticed that a lot of black people stink?"

I grew up hearing these racial slurs, and I encounter them in the sports arena and the corporate world to this day. In order to keep my wits about me, I've had to train myself not to feel threatened by bigots. This did not come easily to me, because as a kid, I always had an impulse to blow up. In the neighborhood I lived in, everybody blew up. That's the way we communicated. My mother wanted me to be polite, but if I tried to express things in a calm way, people didn't understand me.

"Y'know, that really hurts my feelings. Maybe you should try to . . ." was always rudely interrupted by, "Aw, shut up!"

Whenever I tried to talk reasonably, my attempt was immediately squashed. I'm not implying that you don't find gentle, soft-spoken individuals and families in the inner cities, but grinding poverty in the land of plenty does deprive people of some of the common civilities that we generally take for granted. You are forced to conform to the law of the jungle. Rough talk is better understood in confrontational situations. You have to speak that language to be heard.

Today, when I find myself in situations that make me mad, I contain my anger. People in the fencing world frequently tell me the worst things about black people, but I just listen without interrupting them. I try to make them feel comfortable with me and I even try to draw them out. This way they'll tell me everything I want to know. If I respond with anger and indignation, I'll never find out what my enemies really think. As the saying goes, it's good to keep your friends close but your enemies even closer. I have learned how to let people expose their weak spots. What they don't seem to realize is that by speaking to me that way, they are dropping their defenses. They are arming me, giving me a psychological advantage over them that will enable me to defeat them easily in any kind of confrontation.

In my career, I have had the opportunity to travel to many other countries. I've met people from a number of different nations. It is always interesting and rewarding to discover new customs. I've learned to appreciate the rich variety of cultures on our planet. However, there is one aspect common to many cultures that is both strange and deeply rooted: color prejudice. Much has been written about this subject, but when you are repeatedly on its receiving end, it can be deeply saddening and disturbing.

Being half African American and half Japanese in this society, in the United States, I'm considered totally black; the Japanese side of me is not recognized at all. This is the way our culture is. Even if you're ten percent black and ninety percent Japanese, you're still considered black. From what I've seen in my travels, this is the way other cultures operate, too. Whether I live here or in Japan or anywhere else in the world, racism exists.

In too many countries, I found that people of color are looked down upon. Even among people from the same country who speak the same language and share common ancestors you will find that the lighter-skinned ones are favored over their darker-skinned brothers and sisters. Many nonwhite people have been browbeaten into thinking that anything white is right. I know how easy it is to fall into the trap where you become so conditioned that you can only see things one way. It's like the dog who sees your hand coming and cringes because he assumes you're going to beat him, even if you want to pet him. When people suggest to you every day, from the moment of birth, that the dark-skinned race is inferior, it is not difficult to develop a complex about the color of your skin. This explains to me why a lot of African Americans still think negatively about themselves and each other, and why there is so much black-on-black violence. It comes out of a negative mindset.

For a long time, I didn't recognize this complex in myself. When my fencing career took off, I saw that I was able to make it big in a "white sport." I began to feel good enough and smooth enough to overcome any obstacles. I viewed any negative encounters with people as individual unconnected events. Fencing had allowed me to enter into white society, and I had arrived at a peak of sorts. I thought, *Wow, this is the way to be!* This new world seemed to be a much more positive environment than I was accustomed to. It certainly was more peaceful, and there was more money to be made there.

I thought I was immune to the race game. But finally, after studying myself and the world around me a little more closely, I realized that this was not so. I saw that light-skinned blacks were definitely favored in the media and in corporate America. I saw that people felt more threatened by darker-skinned blacks. In America, in South Africa, and around the world, I saw that blacks were categorized according to the shade of their skin. I remembered a confrontation my girl-friend and I had in college when an angry black man came up to us and said, "Look at that nigger hangin' out with a white chick."

People often ask me how I've been able to remain one of the top sabrists in the U. S. for the past twenty-two years. My answer is that being an African American in America gives me the fuel I need. The extra edge comes from all that was missing from my relationship with my father. The more social injustice I see, the more my store of anger against injustice increases. I have an ax to grind. There is no question in my mind that ninety-five percent of my success and longevity in fencing comes from the fact that fencing is where I channel all my anger.

Pure anger is pure energy: used correctly, it increases your capability and strength. But sometimes anger can just burst out without warning. It is unhealthy to go through life without checking that tendency. I owe it to fencing that my life wasn't destroyed by this strongest of emotions. The sport requires you to anticipate every move of your opponent, which in turn requires great concentration. The skills of concentration and analysis that I have developed have taught me not to let my anger become a controlling factor, but rather to keep it as a reservoir of energy that I can use to my advantage.

I have become a controlled explosion. Instead of letting my anger be an agent of disruption to my family and friends, I am able to turn it into a positive resource. Mind you, I am speaking in very broad terms and not suggesting that I never lose my cool. Still, I seem to be moving in the right direction. I have learned to walk away from senseless conflict. I see strength, not weakness, in someone who has the ability to walk away from macho behavior. Often, walking away from conflict takes more strength than fighting. I hope that someday I will have the strength to follow the example of the prophets in the Bible, who say to their persecutors, "God bless you. I will pray for you." This is surely the best way to be.

The truth can't be imprisoned forever; eventually it will come out. The finest example of this in our lives is Nelson Mandela. Mandela is a compassionate human being, and compassion knows no bounds. When the South African Government imprisoned him as an important resistance leader, he became a moral inspiration to us all. During his years in prison, he never allowed anger or animosity to overcome him. After twenty-six years, the very same government that Mandela had fought against freed him. Then, in the country's first democratic election to include the non-white majority, Mandela was elected president. The miracle that had happened was a true expression of his strength of character.

When I saw my brothers, sprinters John Carlos and Tommie Smith, raise their gloved fists in the black power salute during the 1968 Olympics in Mexico City, I was listening to what the media had to say about the event, and it all sounded very negative. Like many other people, I thought, *How could they go against their country? How could they be so negative?* That's the way most of us felt, and those were the messages the media bombarded us with, as the USOC suspended the sprinters from the team and banned them from the site.

Later, I realized that what the brothers did in Mexico City was very brave. Maybe they didn't choose the best method to get their message across. But if a picture is worth a thousand words, they were sending a picture that screamed, *Hey, there are injustices being done to black people in America, and it's a crime! The situation has to change!* They were not being unpatriotic when they used the podium to make that statement. Rather, they were risking their careers to remind America to honor her own founding principles of equality.

One of the great things about our country is the constitutional right of freedom of expression. Much that is good in the USA is based on this fundamental right. Other countries in the same situation might have dealt with their athletes more harshly. But back in 1968, I did not understand this. I felt that these black Olympians were jeopardizing their careers and sending out a militant message about African Americans that didn't represent my own views. This, coupled with my one-track mind about training and fencing my way out of the ghetto, added up to one badly misinformed guy.

When a person is one-track-minded, he doesn't see things clearly. People who must put all their energy into just surviving often get confused. Politicians get a lot of mileage out of people's confusion. This is how they make mincemeat out of the principles of democracy. People can become so inundated with the pressures of their daily lives that they can be duped easily by anyone. People with low self-esteem can also be manipulated easily. From the perspective of a confused mind, everything appears confused. The world takes on a yellow tint when you are infected with yellow fever. As soon as you are cured, the world looks the way it does to healthy people. You may not like what you see, but it will be closer to the truth.

It took me a long time to get out of my one-sided confusion. But it didn't happen on its own. I had to work at it. My experience with therapy in college gave me a foundation for self-examination, and from that time on, I was determined to understand my mind and my emotions. I bought countless books on psychology, philosophy, and spirituality. Finally, with a lot of time and effort on my part, the fog slowly started lifting.

But the only way to start is to look at yourself first. The way I do this is by asking myself, *What is my weakness? Why am I insecure? How can I stomp on this insecurity and step up to something better?* I tell my students to do this exercise, too. By first looking at ourselves, starting from there to put our best foot forward, we can achieve, one step at a time, something far greater than we would by doing it any other way. This fundamental lesson is not preached often enough. It is a message which has traditionally been passed down by religious leaders, but all of us can use it.

We need to be aware of the illusions created by other people, often politicians, who, like stage magicians, use smoke and mirrors, trumped up statistics, or outright lies to manipulate the truth and tell a one-sided story. Can anyone explain what's going on today with unemployment, unequal distribution of wealth, inadequate housing and health care, the deterioration of our educational systems, the lack of opportunities available to masses of people, and the shameless attempts to sell prisons to private individuals as investment opportunities? Why are there so many black people in jail? Why are Americans so fearful and uptight about each other? In order to get a handle on these issues, we need to be able to distinguish between truth and fiction. Only then can we start dealing with issues of freedom and personal

power. Then, even if we are inundated with family responsibilities, job obligations, or intense training and study, there
will be no turning back.

The mass movement that stood up to slave drivers, conical
white hoods, smoking guns, and snarling attack dogs helped
to create a new generation of African Americans who are
proud of their African heritage, both culturally and geneti-
cally. African Americans now have a greater understanding and
appreciation of their history. The effect of this movement on
the churches, educational institutions, and arts and humanities in our country has been irreversibly positive and profound.

It took me decades to fully appreciate the courage our
black leaders needed to face down racism wherever they saw
it. Martin Luther King and Malcolm X were brave individuals who realized that death held no dominion over them. In
a society so intensely geared toward personal gain, they actually put their lives on the line to further a cause that would
improve the lives of millions. They achieved that goal to a
certain extent. But the struggle, every bit as patriotic as red,
white and blue, continues. Black History Month, with its corporate sponsorship, is a step in the right direction, helping
to make all Americans aware of the African-American contribution to our country.

Let us not forget that many of these contributions have
been nothing short of brilliant. What is too often conve-
niently forgotten, and overlooked in school curriculums, is
the fact that African Americans have produced some of the
greatest builders, educators, inventors, farmers, soldiers, and

pilots—not to mention fencers—in this country and around the world. We have broken countless records in sports and music. And everyone knows that African-American people have always kept America and the rest of the world dancing.

My younger black Olympian fencing brothers Bob Cottingham and Michael Lofton are part of the generation that grew up with positive black values. They helped me to be more aware of who I am as an African American. I am also indebted to my wife, Susann, a longtime Harlem resident.

I had been living in my Greenwich Village apartment for ten years before I met Susann. It was 1987, and Susann was living in Harlem with her eight-year-old son, Dorian. She loved it there. I had been reluctant to move uptown, associating Harlem with the poverty I grew up with in Newark. But she finally convinced me to join her. It wasn't long before I discovered that despite the risk of violence that exists there, Harlem has a remarkably strong community spirit. In Susann's building, I exchanged pleasantries and warmth with more people in one week than I did in ten years in my building in Greenwich Village. There is an abundance of beauty, love of life, and resilience in Harlemites. On the streets and among the beautiful old buildings are generations of role models that boys and girls like me never knew existed. You can see a lawyer next to a homeless man, a surgeon next to a crackhead, an angry teenager next to a college president. People at a disadvantage exist side-by-side with people who are leading exemplary lives. Most important of all, I discovered the quiet pride of being black that has existed in Harlemites for generations.

Once I was exposed to the relaxed feeling of living in Harlem with Susann, it wasn't long before I discovered The Abyssinian Baptist Church under the aegis of Reverend Dr. Calvin O. Butts III, who continues to inspire me every Sunday. I am only too happy to confess that my experiences in Harlem have been a kind of rehabilitation for me. They have introduced me to a rich culture that was absent for the first thirty-five years of my life. For too many years of my adulthood, I had let go of my roots. Spending all of my time in the corporate world and the world of fencing meant that most of my time was spent with whites. Now I see the value of living among my own people. There's so much shared experience in this community—it's something that I wouldn't be able to get anyplace else. I am certain that living in a positive black environment helps me to communicate and contribute not only to black people, but to our society as a whole.

A STRONG FOUNDATION 10

In 1987, my friend Tom Shepard, a talented entrepreneur and businessman, suggested that we organize a fencing clinic for inner-city kids. Initially, my reaction was, *All I need to do with my time now is to teach a bunch of unruly, snotty-nosed kids how to fence! And why would they want to learn a white European sport traditionally practiced by elite members of society anyway?* In the back of my mind, I knew there was something to be said for Tom's idea, but I was busy training for the '88 Olympics and mentoring was not a big priority for me. As time went on, however, my point of view began to change. My competitive career had lasted longer than most, and fate was still smiling on me. I realized that I'd been given so much I simply had to give back. If it meant I had to suffer a little, so what? It was time.

The Peter Westbrook Foundation was officially launched in February 1991 at the New York Fencers Club on West 71st Street in Manhattan. I viewed the venture as an opportunity to teach inner-city kids life skills. I wanted to teach them how to win and lose, deal with stress, control their emotions, and strive for excellence.

On that first wintry Saturday in February, we had six kids, all of them our own relatives or those of our friends. The next Saturday, forty little black, brown, white, and yellow faces showed up at the club, and no one could believe it. People thought I was crazy. Everybody told me that within two weeks we'd lose two-thirds of the kids. We didn't lose any. Parents came to us and said that they couldn't understand it. They had never seen their kids get involved with any activity as passionately as they took to fencing.

My partners and I weren't surprised. We understood what was going on. These kids were not so different from us. We had grown up in the inner city too, a place where kids fight each other all the time. Since fencing is a combat sport, the transition from life to fencing is a very natural one for kids from this kind of background. What did surprise me was my own change in attitude. The kids had an effect on me that is hard to describe. Working with them brought me in touch with a feeling of joy that was new to me and overwhelming.

We started out with a core group of staff members that included medalists and Olympians: Michael Lofton, a NYU graduate and publicist by profession; Robert Cottingham, a Columbia graduate and attorney; and Donald Anthony, a Wharton graduate and video producer. Members of the core group were amazingly self-motivated about sharing the responsibilities of running the foundation. They were my spiritual brothers, my partners in every way. Mike was the computer man and letter writer, Bob took care of all the legal matters, and Don managed the financial end of the operation. It is significant that my partners were all highly competent and well-rounded African-American males, supposedly a rare commodity in our culture. Yet here we were starting out with the best in the business. Our board of directors also boasted the best in the business, including former NYU President John Brademas and champion athletes Wilma Rudolph and Arthur Ashe. All in all, it seemed that the foundation was simply meant to be.

Very quickly, the program snowballed. The numbers in our coaching crew grew with the number of kids joining the program. Olympic coaches Csaba Elthes and fellow Hungarian Aladar Kogler, illustrious fixtures at the club, were so taken by the spirit and energy of our Saturday morning sessions that they both asked if they could be part of the already formidable team that had assembled almost overnight. Later we received among our ranks foilist Eric Rosenberg, assisted by Olympic prospect Herb Raynaud. Eric was running his own program for young fencers, which he now combined with ours, bringing his ten white youngsters into our fold. Soon after, the Cuban Olympian sabrist Lazarro Mora joined in, along with Ukrainian Yuri Gelman and Afro-Cuban Max Catala. To add to our multicultural crew, we now get energetic help from Russian coach Boris Leiberman and from Haitian Rotchild Magloire.

The foundation's mission is "Development of the Individual through Fencing." Through fencing, the program seeks to open up avenues to a higher level of personal development and to give the child an alternative to traditional extracurricular activities. The fencing experience enriches and develops the child's mind and body through rigorous discipline. Our program not only seeks to create Olympic fencers, but to teach children to excel academically, to manage their emotions, and to become contributing members of our society. Excellence is no accident. We encourage our young people to strive for excellence in all things.

I don't like to turn people down, but the New York Fencers Club can only accommodate about seventy-five pupils, and these days, the house is always full. The kids range in age from nine to seventeen. We begin with basic warm-up exercises and group activities. First we do stretching, then we drill fencing footwork, showing them the basic moves: on-guard (the starting position), advance, retreat, lunge, and fleche (the running attack). Then we teach them the hand skills, the basic hands, no weapons. Next we bring in the weapons and masks and gloves and jackets. We keep and maintain our own supply. The atmosphere is charged with excitement. Quite a few parents sit through the entire three-hour session every Saturday morning.

After that, we give equal time to each student individually. The most gifted and disciplined students are channeled into an elite training program. These kids quickly become dedicated and show up for training several times a week. We sponsor the most advanced pupils at various domestic and international competitions. Each fencer develops at his or her own pace because each trains individually with a coach. The differences between the students' skills show up during matches. These competitive sessions serve to drive the slower students to try harder and to pay more attention. As coaches, we try to identify and work through their weak points.

Every Saturday morning before the class begins, Bob Cottingham shows the kids a half-hour reel of some useful documentary with his old-fashioned, whirring, eight-millimeter film projector. In addition to fencing, to take advantage of the large gathering of young people, we also invite speakers as often as we can. They talk to the kids about what they do, answer a lot of questions, and help to demystify their professions by letting the kids know how they got there. We've had educators, engineers, lawyers, sports professionals, doctors, corporate executives, and radio and television producers come in to speak. Not always, but often, they are black people who come from inner-city backgrounds. This way the kids can see that these professions are not reserved for white or yellow people or for people with privileged upbringings. The students get an expanded sense of the possibilities that exist for each of them.

When I started the foundation, I wasn't convinced that inner-city youth in this country would appreciate fencing, because they're so bombarded with conventional sports on TV, big money sports like basketball, baseball, football, and boxing. I really thought it would be a waste of my valuable time and energy. I thought it would deplete my spiritual energy. The reality turned out to be completely contrary to my original belief.

I find that I look forward to going and changing these kids' lives every Saturday. We have between eighty and one hundred students now, and I actually see the difference our involvement makes. They're so excited about the fencing program that they bring boundless enthusiasm to it. The parents tell me that they see changes in their kids' attitudes towards African-American role models, school work, and in their interactions with people from all walks of life. For those who attend classes more than once a week, we notice an even greater effect on their interpersonal skills since we have a chance to be around them more often and can provide more guidance.

The current update on the performance of our students in the fencing arena is that the kids are unbelievable. We don't put them in tournaments until they're exceptional, and exceptional many of them are. In 1996, Erinn Smart and Kari Coley made both the under-seventeen and the under-twenty world championship teams. But in January 1997, like Aki Spencer-El did the previous year, Errin outdid herself by placing first in the U. S. National tournament. Katie Cavan, at the age of fourteen, became the youngest fencer ever to place third in a world championship tryout, adding to the ranks of foundation youth who have proven to be among the finest fencers in the land.

We also have a minimum of four people representing the United States of America and the Peter Westbrook Foundation at the junior world championships. In 1995, these tournaments were held in Paris, and in '96 they were held in Belgium.

In order to sharpen the skills of these competitors, the foundation has been flying them abroad. This was not in my original plan, but I've realized that if they're going to compete on world championship and Olympic teams, they need to experience the international environment. I've taken five of our contestants to Budapest, Hungary. Next I plan to take four people to Germany.

I've been working very closely with two of our future Olympians for a number of years. Keeth Smart has been with me since we started the foundation back in 1991, and Aki Spencer-El came on board in 1993. They're both seventeen, but they're as different as can be. Keeth is tall and lean and unusually well-mannered. He has just been accepted at St. John's University on a fencing scholarship. Aki is like a tough young gangster—a fighter and martial artist whose roughness shows in everything about him. My wife discovered Aki in the Harlem Little League and urged his mother to bring him to the foundation. Now he's so crazy about fencing that he's given up everything else.

Keeth and Aki have come a long way since I first met them. I feel like their older brother. We travel together, share hotel rooms, and trade personal stories. I try to bring out their best qualities, not only as fencers but as human beings. I love the way they listen to me. When I talk, their big rabbit ears go straight up! I'm as proud of their successes as a parent. Their performance at school has improved, and their fencing skills are terrific. Recently Keeth placed second in the senior Olympic trials by beating Mike Lofton, Dave Mandell, and Don Anthony—all of whom are veteran champions. Aki made the finals in another senior Olympic trial by defeating several past Olympians, including me! He placed first in the national tryouts, securing his position on the U. S. Senior

World Championship Team. Aki had been fencing a mere three years. Keeth and Erinn Smart had placed second and third in similar tryouts.

These examples are not flukes, but results of a truly high-level program that is creating future Olympians and role models. Athletes who make the Olympic team are strong and powerful men and women in their late teens and early twenties. Our hopefuls are still too young, but they need to go to all the Olympic trials to be ready for what lies ahead. And if any of them *does* make it to an Olympic team at such a tender age, it will certainly set a precedent.

We want our students to excel in school as well as on the fencing strip, so the foundation has become much stricter than at the outset about academic standing. Parents talk to us about how their kids are doing in school, and we try to level directly with kids who are having problems. For members of the elite program, we actually monitor their report cards and, on occasion, speak with their school teachers. If anyone is having a hard time with a particular subject, we have fifteen paid tutors who give the students one-on-one instruction. Year round, the tutors are prepared to meet the kids on whatever weekday or weekend is mutually convenient. They spend an hour or two with these students on a regular basis, helping them to understand concepts and prepare for tests, usually in the areas of math, science, and English. Within a semester, C and D students have progressed to being B students. Tutoring makes the difference.

The Peter Westbrook Foundation started out with six kids, and over the last five years nearly one thousand kids have come through our doors. The United States Olympic Committee has recognized our commitment to the children of New York by granting us $35,000 in each of the past three years. The funds are managed by Dr. Alpha Alexander of the YWCA, an indefatigable defender of our cause. In turn, we give fencing demonstrations all over the country, especially on the East Coast and at New York City public schools. We've also helped the New York City Parks & Recreation Department start their own fencing program.

During the winter of 1995, I spoke before a United States Senate Hearing in Washington, D. C. The senators had called in the United States Olympic Committee to see if they'd made good on their promise to promote and nurture competitive athletes in the inner city. In response, the USOC cited the Peter Westbrook Foundation and presented me. I spoke as a witness representing the United States Olympic Committee about the work of my foundation. Afterwards, several senators informed me that they were proud to hear about the good job we were doing. I'm proud that the foundation is getting public recognition in so many different spheres.

The USOC has been the significant shot in the arm in terms of funding for our foundation. Prior to receiving its support, most of our donations were from private corporations and individuals. Sometimes we would earn a bit of money by doing demonstrations or through donation drives. Stacey Johnson, vice president of the USFA and a member of the USOC nominating committee, also got us some funding. She testified at the Congressional hearing that my example had given her the courage to start her own program. She said she didn't realize before we came along that this kind of program could be run without having millions of dollars. She now runs an inner-city program in San Antonio, Texas.

Still, fundraising is an ongoing struggle. The foundation bears all the expenses of running the school. We pay for private lessons, fencing equipment, and air fares to tournaments around the country and abroad. Thanks to all our benefactors and patrons, I am in the position to pay the staff small gratuities. We hope that as the word about the foundation spreads, the media and private individuals will keep contacting us with their support. *Sports Illustrated* asked us to do a fencing demonstration for their *"Sports Illustrated for Kids Day"* in New York, and gave us a small fee. Whatever we earn from such invitations we plow back into the foundation. I know that with God's help we will be able to support our program for a long time to come.

Our inner-city youth is an untapped resource. African Americans, Latinos, Whites, Asians, whoever. This resource has been neither utilized nor encouraged. I've proven that this category of people, people like me, can be a precious asset to society. Olympians can be created from kids off the street, not just from private club members and university students. There are a lot more people out there who can bring us gold and glory. It is tragic to see our society overlooking precisely the segment of the population that needs looking into to heal the malaise that afflicts our country. I hope that in my lifetime, many more opportunities will come to the inner city, and that we will all see a great change there.

MENTORING BASICS 11

Mentoring young people can be the most frustrating and the most gratifying of experiences. I don't consider myself to be an authority on mentoring or on education. But through the work of my foundation, I have learned a few important lessons about motivating young adults to discover higher levels of capabilities within themselves. I know that it is not only the students and their conditions that govern the outcome of our efforts. As parents and mentors, our greatest challenge is to outgrow our own limitations. We need to develop enough self-awareness not to pass on our own faults. Only then can we empower young people to overcome the obstacles blocking their growth. Change is a positive force for everyone: the mentor, the student, and the community. With every breakthrough, the whole group progresses.

In any situation, when faced with a seemingly insurmountable problem, we can't hope for a solution unless we are willing to look at that problem in a radically different way. To use a metaphor, the key is in the lock but it needs turning to unlock it. What if we were to assume the attitude that the problem provides us with an opportunity to discover the secret to our own liberation? Why else would it be there? It is not my intention to make light of a complex subject, but rather to share my observations with the hope that they may help someone unhappily trapped in a negative state of mind.

Never underestimate the simple power of love and kindness. Show affection. Kids love being hugged and kissed. Who doesn't? Put your arms around them and talk to them often. Give them your undivided attention. Try to lift their spirits. Use encouraging words to demonstrate your support. I always try to tell the kids what a good job they're doing. People need that in life. This is one of the things we endeavor to provide at the foundation.

Find out what kids are willing to work for, what turns them on. I've learned that while the parents of many of our students hope that fencing will lead to college scholarships, the kids aren't thinking about their education at all. But the idea of making the Olympics—now *that's* another matter! Once I've figured out what motivates them and have gotten their interest, I teach them how to set and achieve goals. I show them the tangible progress that results from training, and how the more time they put in, the better they become. I explain how they can achieve the same kind of progress by applying these principles in school and in their personal lives.

Many young people are in a negative state of mind when they first come to the fencing classes. It's amazing to see what a little encouragement at the right moment can do for them. It can affect their whole personality. When I see them making progress, I congratulate them publicly and privately. In some of the kids I've known for a few years, I see an incredible change. Now that they are teenagers, they talk to me about their lives and relate to me as a friend. I remember when Rashaan Greenhouse first came to the club, he told me he was uncomfortable training with so many white people. I told him that he was not alone. He's not the only person who has ever felt that way. In fact, I'd had the same experience myself. I found that simply sharing with Rashaan the pain and anxiety that I'd felt in similar situations seemed to help him.

Whenever an occasion arises, I try to impress upon our kids the benefits of the giving spirit. We've had a few incidents at the club where certain locker room possessions—subway tokens, a driver's license, my brand new Tommy Hilfiger shirt—have suddenly gone missing. I let the students know in no uncertain terms that their deeds will come back to them. To reinforce the point, I reward them for coming forth with the truth.

A lot of kids go berserk when they lose. I explain to them that I've lost many times. Often they seemed quite surprised to learn this. Still other kids feel guilty about whacking their friends and family with swords during practice sessions at the foundation. I tell them that in this environment, you're allowed to beat your friends and family. You can give them a hug *after* you beat them.

When I first started to teach fencing, I was kind of terse with the kids. On a couple of occasions when some kids became a little rambunctious, I grabbed them and shook them up a bit. My attitude used to be, *Hey, listen. I'm putting myself out to do this, and these kids are being unappreciative. They're wasting my time.* Then it dawned on me that this was the wrong approach to take. Now I'm much more tolerant and patient. My job is to support them, not to shake them up just as society so rudely does. It's the pecking order of our social system: the president rattles the vice-president, the vice-president shakes down the manager, the manager yells at the employee, the employee comes home and abuses his wife, and then the wife takes it out on the children who kick the dog. I was a part of that social order. So now I'm more aware of the shake-down. No more shake-downs! Instead, I endeavor to lift them up. Today, those same problem kids are a great source of joy for us. I have learned that forbearance is much more productive than the shake-down.

This position has helped me in other areas of my life, too. For example, when I walk down the street, I can look at the drug dealer and say, "How ya' doin'?" I still have the impulse to take his head off, but I choose to take another approach.

I talk to kids on the street who have no self-respect, joking around with them and putting a little love in their life. "Hey, you guys wanna play videos? Come on. I'll give you guys a dollar. Let's go and play video games." It doesn't take much to put a little love and a little reaching out into their lives.

I see plenty of kids who act like they are going nowhere soon. When they see me walking down the street they call out, "Hey, you're the guy that does the fencing. You're the guy that knows karate. Show us your fencing moves. Show us your karate moves." So I show them a few moves. It means a little something because it shows that someone is taking an interest in their lives. It's not much, but it may help out.

My friend Alison Thomas-Cottingham, a doctor of child psychology and the wife of my partner Bob Cottingham, conducted a study among African Americans of all socio-economic backgrounds and found that the quality of support children receive is a key factor in their development. In fact, she believes that receiving the right kind of support is the key to a person's success.

Alison's parents own a grocery store. They never went to college. I asked her how she wound up with a Ph.D.

"I was very fortunate," she explained. "My mother pushed me in the academic direction when I was a very young kid. She made me take special courses and she put me in private schools. I had no time to hang around kids who were not doing that. If I had, I would probably be more athletic and a much better dancer, but I'd also have the same problems as everybody else."

Another good example is my friend Lettice Selama.Weit. She is an African American and a single mother raising a daughter in New York City. She had always been very single-minded about steering her daughter, Desirée, in the direction of intellectual pursuits. At the age of nine, Desirée's reading level was that of a college student's. Her achievement certainly puts to rest those theories about "inborn deficiencies."

Then there's the case of my colleague Don Anthony. Although Don's athleticism is very strong, his intellect and general knowledge are also well above average by any standard. Don's graduation score at The Wharton School of Business was among the top ten in the whole country. Actually, the people at Wharton didn't even understand how Don managed to graduate, as he was always traveling around the world to tournaments and fencing with me. The rest of the students were in school eight hours a day, and he was there maybe eight hours in a week. Don assured me it was not the case that he was smarter than everyone else. He was simply familiar with the system and was not intimidated by it.

"My mother knew to expose me to things at an early age that a majority of African Americans are not exposed to," Don explained. "She had me taking tests before I was eight years old. At a very young age, I was taking courses on how to take tests, and how to study effectively to score high on them. You learn how to weed out useless information and concentrate on the essentials. I was training at a very young age to develop skills in reading and writing. And that's why I'm good at it. Most Americans, let alone African Americans, are really not exposed to that kind of training, and that's why my peers didn't succeed as well as I did."

It is so important to expose our children to different experiences early on in life. A child living in a multilingual society with more than one language being taught in school will grow up speaking several languages. In our country most kids barely speak one language with much confidence. In Amsterdam, where every kid is taught Dutch, English, and

French, all kids, white and black, speak three languages. If you go to any African or Asian city you'll be amazed to find how many people speak several languages. It is almost shocking to see how pliable and quick to learn young minds are, given the right setting. Take a six-year-old black child to China and see how fast the kid learns Chinese. Necessity makes us learn, and we learn faster when we are younger.

Periodically our academic institutions and media jungles throw up writers who cash in on ignorance and fear-laden small-mindedness. They make bestsellers by pushing the myth that whites are more intelligent than blacks. Citing biased, culture-specific intelligence tests, these writers claim that whites are better endowed than blacks *by nature* to comprehend intellectual concepts, while blacks make superior athletes and sportsmen. I don't know if it's racism, or a case of people just accepting what they've always heard, or a case of too many people not really thinking for themselves, but believe it or not, a lot of people, white and black, believe this.

I can understand how it might appear that African Americans are superior in sports. Even my coaches—white coaches, Eastern European Anglo coaches—seemed to feel that African Americans are naturally superior in athletics. This is a gross generalization of the facts. My position is that if you believe African Americans are better than everybody else at sports, you are also buying into the idea that it is possible for one racial group—in this case the white one—to be better at intellectual pursuits. This idea is hard to swallow for several reasons. First, in our increasingly mixed society, the genetic components of "race" are constantly in a state of flux. Then consider the fact that in Europe the most talented athletes are white. The inferiority of blacks was always used to justify Europe's colonial ventures. The physical superiority of blacks is just the other side of the same coin. It is simply a perpetuated myth.

There are countless numbers of African Americans who have left their mark on America in fields other than sports and entertainment. Several of them have recently been featured in a series of U. S. postage stamps called "I Have a Dream." From the culinary arts to whaling to literature, one can read their biographies. All you have to do is go to the library and ask. If you get really curious, go to the Schomburg Center for Research in Black Culture in Harlem. They have the archiving of Black Americana down to a science. The point is that there are many thousands of us making a living as neurobiologists, software developers, beauticians, senators, architects, upholsterers, inventors, stock brokers, electricians, astronomers, museum curators, pilots, dog groomers—clearly the list could be as long as the number of professions in the world. The millions of people who do great work behind the scenes just aren't as visible as high-profile sports players, who are really just the same few people presented by the media over and over again.

I see elements both within and outside African-American culture that push many of our people toward careers in athletics. The recognition of talent and the generous monetary rewards attract the best of us into professional sports. Our need to prove our excellence in a venue other than the United States Armed Forces, and the fact that few areas are

open to us in a shrinking job market, may also explain why
we produce so many athletic geniuses. It is equally true that
African Americans tend to be good dancers. For thousands
of years traditional African cultures have employed rhythm
and dance as a vital socializing and harmonizing factor. Our
culture has always emphasized physical competition. And
since so many black men and women have become world-
famous personalities by excelling in sports and entertainment,
our people are quick to encourage those traits in their young
ones. It all stems from our values, our culture, and what we
are exposed to. It works the same way whether you're black
or white. There's always so much more promise when one's
ability is looked upon favorably.

We all need to cultivate the ability to mentor others. By exam-
ining how our relationships with our parents formed during
childhood and the ways in which they conditioned us, we
might begin to free ourselves of the idiosyncrasies that have
been handed down to us. There's a lot of truth to the saying
that the cuckoo calls its own name. When we are teaching
children, no matter how great we think we are, it behooves
us to remember that we are always operating from a very limited store of knowledge and experience. Obstacles and problems arise because of the limitations of our own perception
more than they do because of the kids' limitations.

Kids are so delicate and intricate and sacred. It has taken
me a while to really understand that. I approached my first
mentoring experiences thinking that with my views, my
knowledge, my experience, my expertise, I was bringing a

hell of a lot to the table. But there's another big factor that I didn't see at the time, which is what the kids bring to the table. What do I know about their scars and their experience, how their parents relate to them, what kind of an environment they're being raised in? There are so many details. I may have had a lot of skills, but that was only the half of it in dealing with kids. So now I try to be a little more open and receptive, not such a know-it-all. I try to see and hear their stories, their past, where they come from, and then try to guide and shape and help them.

My experience as a mentor really began with my relationship with my stepson, Dorian. Dorian came into my life when he was eight years old—he's seventeen now. When we first met, I showered him with affection, but I was operating blindly. I thought I had all the answers and could solve every problem. I wanted to make him a model citizen and a model child. I tried to jam everything I knew down his throat. But I was not looking at who he was. I wish I could have given him then some of what I know now. Today, Susann and I are very curious to see who Dorian will become as an adult, how he'll put the great puzzle of life together for himself. Let's see what kind of a Picasso he can come up with.

How can I possibly be an agent for change in others if I can't renew myself? Like all skills, this too can be developed through careful practice. We need to be able to recognize our negative patterns and to ask, *What am I doing to perpetuate this?* When caught up in a vicious cycle, we should be able to stop in our tracks, recollect, reconsider the overall picture, reset our minds just like a personal computer, and re-boot. The secret is to change both one's attitude and one's actions. It has become very clear to me that in order to change, I have to shed my old ways the way a snake sheds its skin. I know that my personal breakthroughs can lead to other people's triumphs, and when that happens, greater good will result.

Careers in professional athletics don't last more than a fraction of a lifetime. Still, athletes who have been in the spotlight can make a big difference in many people's lives. When you're that well-known and you reach out to help people with your time, your money, your energy, and your expertise, the word will spread like wildfire. Now you are inundated with your sport and you don't really have the time to do as much as you would like. But after your career has peaked, you can go on to spread good will, nurture our youth, and change their lives for the better.

Arthur Ashe, who contributed his energy and time to so many grassroots programs, was giving back to the community until his last days. All of us at the foundation were deeply moved when, less than a month before he died of AIDS-related complications, he showed up at our trophy-giving ceremony. I didn't realize at the time how sick he really was.

Arthur called me up before the event and said, "Pete, I really don't feel too great. I'm awfully tired . . . "

I said, "Arthur, I already told the kids you'd be here. Just come over here and give out the medals and show your face, because the kids really are waiting for you."

Now I realize how hard it must have been for him to get out of his bed to come over and do that for us. It was only later that I got the full impact of this man's incredible dedication to people. What great strength and desire he must have had to walk that walk. He showed up looking a bit frail, but not once did he let on that he was in pain or discomfort. He made us feel special. And he made our children feel pretty special. It turned out to be his last public appearance.

It is awesome to consider how many different causes Arthur Ashe found time for. In addition to looking after his own family and his tennis clinics, Arthur gave of himself in a clear and studied manner, whether he was in South Africa with Nelson Mandela or at the White House with the American president or presenting trophies at an inner-city program like ours. He espoused and spoke for some ten to fifteen African-American causes. I couldn't understand how someone could have so much energy. I had always perceived him as the strong, silent type. But he was not so silent when it came to important things. He started an association called the 4As, the African-American Athletic Association, which encourages black people to create their own networks. Each board member pitched in a hundred dollars to start it up. It's kind of like a switchboard for accessing professionals who happened to be African American. We have so much expertise to share with one another and with our children, and this organization is helping us to do that. Now the 4As is raising thousands of dollars in scholarship money for college-bound athletes who have demonstrated academic excellence.

Failure to commit to something other than one's personal interest can jeopardize real peace and contentment. For over a decade, I had more medals, money, and women than I knew what to do with. But somehow I was still frustrated and depressed. My deepest wishes remained unfulfilled and I felt empty inside. It was no joke. Then I realized, *something's wrong. I'm missing something.* Once I turned my life over to helping, so many of my problems simply vanished. Today I operate at a much higher level than I used to. Worlds I had never imagined opened up, not just for me but for hundreds of other people. It makes me happy that other lives are touched through my actions. The business of giving is not a chore when you are doing it with the right attitude. Life is about giving. Yet too many of us still don't give.

Being helpful became my credo with whomever I came in contact with. Love is the supreme message and the only one that counts. Nobody teaches us that in school. Our whole capitalistic culture seems to be telling us: Get for yourself. Get your degree. Get your money. Get your home. Get your gold medal. Go for yourself first. Don't be concerned about giving. Go for yourself, as opposed to, Go and give, and all will be given to you. Now I am happy to give up things that I don't really need—not all of them, but most of them. This attitude allows me to give more to our youth. It is fulfilling my inner need and allowing me to grow. Unless we get out into the world and start giving something useful to people, we're missing out on so much in life. The real deal is giving to people—giving to your brothers, helping your sisters. When you do that, God will reward you ten times over and you will have everything you need. My prayer is that what I'm saying will help make others see that.

DISCOVERIES IN LOSS

12

My mother, Mariko-san Westbrook, passed away on January 2, 1994 at 3:30 p.m. My sister and I were by her side. I'm glad it didn't happen on New Year's Day. Mom died four days after being attacked on a bus and thrown out onto the street. Her head slammed against the sidewalk, and she went into a coma from which she never recovered.

The incident took place close to where she lived near downtown Newark. My mother was on a bus, coming home from shopping at some after-Christmas sales. There were about a dozen people on the bus. Mariko sat next to an old man in the front of the bus, up near the driver. A large African-American woman, maybe twenty years old and 200 pounds, got on the bus with her child. Mom told the black woman with the kid, "Take the scarf off your neck and put it around your child's neck because she's going to catch a cold." The black woman said, "Mind your fucking business. It's my kid."

My mother told the black woman, "It doesn't make any difference. I love all kids."

The two women continued to argue, and then the 200-pound woman went over and started beating up my mother. She wouldn't stop punching and kicking my helpless mother, who was still seated. The bus driver, who was watching everything through the rear-view mirror, did nothing whatsoever to put a stop to the madness. He just kept on driving. Later, he actually denied that he had witnessed a fight.

My mother tried to escape from the still-moving bus while the passengers just looked on. Nobody wanted to get involved. Finally the bus stopped, and when the doors opened, my mother, using her shopping bag to protect her face from the madwoman, took a kick in her stomach. This sent her flying off the bus. Witnesses said that when she hit her head against the edge of the concrete sidewalk and started bleeding, she was stunned. For a second she came to and screamed, "Ah, the pain!" and then she went unconscious. She never spoke again.

Mariko was admitted to the University Hospital Medical Center. Fortunately, she had my sister Vivian's business card on her. The admitting form stated, "Unknown Asian woman. Approximately fifty-five years old." Actually, she was sixty-five.

The hospital caller told my sister, "We have an unidentified Asian woman who is not able to speak, and she has your business card in her pocket. Do you know her?"

"Oh my God, that's my mother!" Vivian said.

She was advised to come down to the hospital immediately. Vivian called me from her office in West Hartford, Connecticut to tell me the news, and I was at my mother's bed-side with my wife, Susann, in half an hour. Vivian arrived shortly afterwards.

As Vivian remembers, "I was driving into Newark, and the worst things I could imagine were racing through my mind. When I got to the hospital, I rushed to the emergency room. I was told that Mom had been taken into surgery immediately because a CAT scan showed bleeding. They told me which floor she was on.

"I got off the elevator, turned down the hallway, and saw my brother and his wife, Susann. I read the looks on their faces. They weren't hopeful.

"When I was in hearing distance, Peter spoke rapidly. 'Mommy's gonna die...she's in a coma...they had to remove part of her brain...there's no hope.'

"I stayed at the hospital day and night. I wanted to be with her. I only left to go to my mother's house to change. Peter also stayed at Mom's house the last two nights. She lived about ten minutes from the hospital. We had given them instructions not to resuscitate, but they would keep her on life support until there was no brain stem activity. So throughout the four days it was pretty much waiting, watching the monitor, waiting for the blood pressure to fall, the heart rate to fall, and everything to flatten."

Looking at my mother in a coma brought me face-to-face with mortality. Mom seemed to have journeyed to the cross-roads of life and death, and paused there. The respirator was the only thing that kept her alive—or was it? The prognosis was that owing to the extensive damage to the brain, she would probably not survive more than a day or two, but she did. To me, that fact was a miracle.

A black nurse at the hospital came up to me and said, "Y'know, I don't care what the doctors say, I have seen situations like this many times." She told me that experience had taught her that patients usually know when their time has come. But they can be reluctant to give up their body if they feel there is something urgent that is left undone. She said she thought my mother would hang on until that unfinished something was completed.

Having never dwelt upon this aspect of the human mystery, my sister and I were really confused. We didn't know what to do for our mother. Her brain was dead but her pulse was steady, and the rest of her systems were functioning. Miraculously, on the fourth day, a woman named Diane McDonald whom we hadn't seen in more than twenty years, came to the hospital. She was a childhood friend of Vivian's, and the only thing I recalled about her was that she used to be on drugs a lot. She came with an older lady. Both had turned their lives over to God. They were able to gain entrance by having nothing more than the Bible in their possession.

The two women came into the room and said a prayer over my mother. When I say prayer, I'm talking about one of those deeply intoned Baptist-Pentecostal prayers. From what I remember, it went something like this: "In the name of Jesus, we rebuke this tragedy; we pray to God that we find the lady who was a disciple of Satan; we pray to God that we find this lady and we pray to God that your soul may rest in peace."

Soon after that prayer, my mother gave up the ghost and

was officially declared dead. To my sister and me, this was an amazing occurrence, a true miracle. We were both relieved when she passed away because we didn't want to see her suffering anymore. I'm not quite sure what significance my mother's religious nature had on it all, but as far as I was concerned, that prayer was a holy final rite. It spoke to me of the existence of a separate and parallel reality that escapes most of us caught up in the pulse of daily life.

Since 1991, Mom had been living by herself. She was lonely, though she would never admit it. She'd become mad when we would tell her that.

"I'm not lonely, I'm just bored!"

Mom was enormously proud of how far I had gotten with my fencing. When she'd hear about my successes, she'd say, "I'm *so* happy, I'm shining mother!" In recent years, however, I knew that she felt it was time for me to move on. "Peter, he big ol' dummyhead," she'd say to Vivian. "Fence, fence, fence, that's all he know!"

Mariko was sixty-five, feisty, and in very good shape. During the last ten years of her life, she spent her time doing missionary work in downtown Newark. She would help feed the homeless, and would buy them food and clothes. It really filled the void of not having a companion, not having anybody to take her around. She was excited every day.

"God, what I did today," she'd say, and then she'd tell me what she did.

Many years before her death, Mom was already preparing for it. She used to tell my sister, "Don't forget, Vivian, I don't want nobody coming to my funeral but you, Peter, Father Yeo, and Father Stalb. That's it."

"I'm going to show your body to everybody!" Vivian would tease her.

"Don't you dare, Vivian. I'm going to come back to get you if you do. I don't want any old body coming and standing over my coffin, looking at my body, talking about me, acting phony, and pretending to have cared for me. Nobody in this world really loves me but you and Peter." She was serious. Vivian asked her if it would be okay to give her a wake. She agreed to that.

When Mom died on a Sunday, we placed an ad in the newspaper announcing that the wake would be held on the following Saturday at a funeral parlor in Newark and that the funeral was private. To carry out Mom's wishes, Vivian arranged to hold the funeral a couple of days later so that people wouldn't follow us to the church after the wake.

At the wake, we had a major turnout. Two rooms were packed with guests. We were so tickled with the response because Mom didn't think that many people loved her. In fact, people were disappointed that the funeral parlor wouldn't reveal the day of the funeral.

As Vivian recalls, "The following Monday, in accordance with Mother's wishes, with only Peter and me present, Father Yeo and Father Stalb presided over the funeral. They both shared in the mass. I felt very good, and as I put my mother in the ground I smiled to myself and thought, *Boy, did you get your wish!*"

Mariko's death was extremely difficult for Vivian and me. Pain spares no one, and the pain of separation that comes after the death of a loved one is one of life's toughest experiences. When we were looking after my mother in the hospital, we met a woman there who told us that she hadn't celebrated Mother's Day in the fifteen years since her mother died. We have to accept the fact that death is a part of life. That means that it's a learning experience. However painful a loss may be, we shouldn't let it weigh us down. It reminds us about the impermanence of all things and the preciousness of life. How can we fully appreciate life if it can be so fleeting? A death can be considered a sad experience or it can be turned into an inspiration. There is no time like now, and death makes you realize that. Until someone close to you dies, you never really understand.

For reasons that are not entirely clear to me, all my life I've been in the habit of blocking out my Japanese side. But things changed after Mariko died. My sister Vivian, who was very close to my mother and lived with her for most of her life, always wanted to know more about our mother's family. Right before Mom's death, Vivian reached out to our relatives in Kobe, and what unfolded may well have been Mariko's parting gift to us.

Mom took three trips to Japan over the years. She always went there alone. If she had really wanted to take us to Japan she would have done so, but she said that she knew the Japanese attitude toward *gaijin*, or outsiders. She said that they even have problems accepting white people, so being African American wouldn't have made things any easier for us. She told us we would be called *kokojin*, a derogatory word that refers to all black people, regardless of whether they have any Japanese blood.

When Mom went into a coma, Vivian called Naohiko Wada, our Japanese cousin, to tell him what had happened. Mom had visited Naohiko and his family a few times in Japan, and they would always send us Christmas cards with family photos and keep in touch with us. In fact, Vivian had spoken with Naohiko in the late '80s when he was working on his doctorate in London. He had invited her to London to visit him there, but at the time, she didn't take him up on the offer. Knowing that Naohiko speaks perfect English, Vivian thought he would be the best person to convey the news to his mother, Mom's older sister, Rosa.

Naohiko and Rosa were shocked by the news, and were very thoughtful and concerned. After Mom passed away, Vivian began to think more about our mother's family. She wanted to establish a new link to our Japanese side. She decided the time was right to visit Naohiko in London.

Naohiko proved to be a warm and worldly artist and performer. His wife, Madeline, is from Lebanon, and they have two children. Naohiko's specialty is Noh theatre, an ancient form of Japanese ceremonial drama. Noh had evolved to become a sort of prayer for peace, longevity, and prosperity for the martial ruling class. Vivian was struck by the ironic coincidence that my cousin and I, descendants of samurai, were both involved in martial arts, though we seem to be approaching the art form from opposite ends of the spectrum—Naohiko as a peacemaker and I as a warrior.

A year later, when Naohiko had a performance engagement at the Smithsonian in Washington, he and his family were able to spend a couple of days in New York before flying back to London. I finally got to meet my Japanese cousins. When they arrived, Vivian, Susann, Dorian, and I took them to the Shark Bar, a really fun soul food restaurant on the Upper West Side. They got their first taste of collard greens, ribs, and Southern fried chicken, and they loved it all.

Naohiko and Madeline have two beautiful kids, a son named Naotomo who is nine, and a daughter named Soraya who is thirteen. They were very open to me. I enjoyed showing them affection and playing around with them, though they always became more formal when their father was around. Soraya told me a little bit about what it was like to be biracial in Japan. She said that people teased her because of her looks. She is not petite, like most Japanese women, and her complexion is much darker than theirs. No matter how hard she tried, she could not meet their standard of beauty. In fact, Soraya is very beautiful, and I made it a point to tell her that in America, her only problem would be keeping all the boys away!

Naohiko told us some incredible family stories. He said that Mariko and Rosa's father, Grandfather Sataro, was rather eccentric and terribly strict. Once he had Mariko and Rosa scrub the whole ceiling of a room with toothbrushes! Such stories helped shed some light on why our mother had such an obsessive edge regarding discipline, which we may well have inherited from her.

He also helped us understand the impact on Mariko of witnessing her mother's horrible death. Of all her siblings—

two brothers and her sister, Rosa—Mariko was the closest to her mother. To make matters even more painful, she also lost one brother to the war, not to mention the destruction of the family's ancestral home and the loss of all their material possessions. Naohiko said that ever since this time, Mariko had been a very nervous person. Even as Vivian and I were growing up, the tragedy continued to plague Mom. Every few years for a short period of time, she would seem to relive the horrors and become terribly depressed, almost to the point of having a nervous breakdown.

As it turned out, our visit with Naohiko and his family was only the beginning of this new relationship with my Japanese side. The following spring, Susann and I finally decided to tie the knot. We sent out wedding invitations to my Japanese relatives strictly as an announcement and a courtesy; we never imagined that they would think to come. So when Naohiko called to inform me that he and his mother would be attending our wedding, I was shocked. Then I realized that it was probably some kind of Japanese thing, this extreme sense of duty. I figured that if I could make him understand that he was off the hook, we'd all feel better. Teasing him just a little, I said "Naohiko, I relinquish you of your obligation."

Naohiko thanked me. He said that he would be honored to attend my wedding, but he had so many things he needed to do in Japan, and the journey would indeed be a long and arduous one for his mother to make. Rosa had only traveled by plane two times in her life. He told me he would let her know that they did not need to come. I was glad we had things squared things away.

Two days later, Naohiko called me again. "Petah, my mother is going to come to your wedding, and I will come with her. She told me that she is getting older now, she may not live forever, you are the link to her beloved sister who is no longer alive, and she must see you before she dies."

Well, it was quite a thrill to have my Japanese relatives at my wedding. Aunt Rosa proved to be quite a striking lady: jewelry, shades, cool, very classy; even at her age she turned heads. I couldn't believe that this 76-year-old Japanese woman spent thirteen hours on a plane just to see me get married. She just wanted to see me and touch me and feel me and spend time with me. I had to say to myself, *Who would do that? Who in their right mind would do that?* That really showed me something.

Now, after spending time with Naohiko and Rosa, I understand what my sister and my relatives were searching for. By reaching out to one another, they found what they were searching for and were satisfied. And, in turn, *I* got satisfied. It gave me something of me that I never had, something that was always missing. So I have that now, that other thing from Japan, that thing I didn't even want to look at. Now I can feel it.

I saw my father for the last time when I was sixteen. He had come up from Florida and I met him at my uncle Olin's house. He asked me again if I wanted to live with him. All I could think about was that this was the same man I had seen physically abusing both my mother and his girlfriend, and who hadn't shown any remorse, even after he recovered from his alcohol-fueled demonic possession. I was full of contempt, and angrily told him I didn't want to have anything to do with him.

What followed was the regrettable culmination of a tragic sequence of misunderstandings on my part. I wound up in a situation that could no longer afford me the opportunity to resolve my anger towards my father. This should serve as a warning to those who believe that stubborn pride or meting out revenge under any circumstances can lead to anything good.

In 1972 when I was in college, my father called me from his hospital bed in Florida. He had suffered a cardiac arrest. He was dying.

His actual words were, "I'm in the hospital and I'm going to die. Peter, can you come and see me before I go?"

Under the cruel grip of stubbornness, I blurted out what had been festering in my heart for so many years. The gist of what I managed to tell him was, "You left me, and now you're telling me to come and visit you because you're dying. That's not a good enough reason for me to go see you."

"Pete, I'm dying. I'll give you a car if you come down," he persisted.

"Is it new?" I asked. I had gotten so callous that I actually thought to myself that maybe I would consider going if he was offering me a new car or a large enough sum of money.

He told me it wasn't. I told him I wasn't coming down either way. To my mind, I heard no apology from my father for his past behavior, and that was not sitting well with me. Ulysses Westbrook died soon after, and I didn't feel a thing.

My mother and sister, who had suffered so much from my father's abuse, were shocked when I refused to go to his funeral. They tearfully begged me to go with them, but I refused. I had made up my mind. I didn't want to have to mask my true feelings at the funeral, pretending to be sad when I wasn't. Although he sired me, I saw my father as an outsider for not being there when I needed him most. He was worse than a stranger to me, and I had no desire to be present at his last rites. My mother and sister went down to the funeral without me.

My father represents to me everything I don't want to be, and yet I am far worse off for not seeing him before his death. In his own way, he knew that it was important for both of us to see each other one last time, but I couldn't bring myself to fulfill his wish. Now I understand that he was a product of his environment, that he had more than his share of insecurities and limitations, and that I have to forgive him. Nevertheless, there is a bitterness and rage that surfaces when I think about my father. It's a part of me, and it propels me to fight. I wonder who I'd be today if I had healed the rift with my father. That part of my life will always remain unresolved. But thank God I have my fencing, because without a place to channel all these feelings, I probably would have imploded a long time ago.

AFTERWORD

In November 1995, I was honored to be among a group of athletes who received a Sports Image Award for our efforts to better our communities, our nation, and our world. The others were Muhammad Ali, Al Attles, Carl Lewis, Dave Stewart, Venus Williams, and Steve Young.

Ali had been a hero to me ever since his 1964 Olympic victory. Now I had a chance to get to know my hero up close. Ali and his wife and Susann and I rode around San Francisco together in a limousine. Ali loved doing tricks and telling jokes. "Hey, Pete, look at this. Watch me levitate." He could actually make it look like he was lifting off the ground. We even got to watch a boxing match together between heavyweight champions Riddick Bowe and Evander Holyfield on TV. The whole experience was magical.

In October 1996, George Steinbrenner and I received the the USOC's F. Don Miller Award for our contribution to amateur athletes. F. Don Miller was president of the Olympic Committee. The award is only given once every four years. I felt so honored to be recognized in this way.

One other important thing happened that fall. The woman who attacked my mother on the bus in New Jersey was charged with aggravated manslaughter and then sentenced to sixteen years in prison.

Now, at the end of my book, you may be wondering what I'm going to do with all my anger since I'm no longer parrying in the competitive fencing arena. This is my plan: I'm going to channel my energies and anger into my work for the foundation, raising money, motivating others through public speaking, and of course, coaching and mentoring and traveling with my kids. I'll still be working out, fencing once in a while, getting involved in other community-minded projects once in a while, but whatever I do, I want to focus on making a difference. Also, I can't ever forget about getting back to the basics: looking at my anger, realizing where it comes from, and making sure that when it comes up, I always find a way to use or diffuse it.

I'm still not an expert at harnessing anger, but at least I know how to make that energy work for me. I'm not as angry as I used to be. I see a lot of people who only get more angry and frustrated as time goes by, until they turn into grumpy old men and women. I'm lucky that I find myself getting more mellow. I find myself able to be in the Zone more often. I'm more appreciative. The only reason I'm not more grouchy, irritable, and unpleasant is that I practice the techniques I've spoken about here. I am definitely a product of what I preach. I see that it works. If you look at your basic foundation, your idiosyncracies, and start to work on that when you're younger, you can actually shed your negative ways. Then, even when you get older and start losing muscle strength, your spiritual strength will continue to grow.

APPENDIX

MAJOR COMPETITIONS, AWARDS, & HONORS

1973   NCAA National Champion, men's sabre

1974   National Champion, men's sabre
       Member, U. S. World Championship team

1975   Bronze individual medal and silver team medal,
           Pan American Games
       National Champion, men's sabre,
       Member, U. S. World Championship team

1976   Member, U. S. Olympic Fencing Team (Montreal)
       First place, Martini & Rossi International Fencing
           Challenge

1978   Member, U. S. World Championship team
1979   Silver team medal, Pan American Games
       National Champion, men's sabre
       Member, U. S. World Championship team

1980   Member, U. S. Olympic Fencing Team (Moscow)
National Champion, men's sabre
USFA Athlete of the Year

1981   National Champion, men's sabre
Member, U. S. World Championship team

1982   National Champion, men's sabre
Member, U. S. World Championship team

1983   Gold individual medal and silver team medal,
    Pan American Games
National Champion, men's sabre
USFA Athlete of the Year

1984   Bronze medal, men's individual sabre,
    U. S. Olympics (Los Angeles)
National Champion, men's sabre
USFA Athlete of the Year

1985   National Champion, men's sabre
Member, U. S. World Championship team
New York University Sports Hall of Fame

1986   National Champion, men's sabre

1987   Silver individual medal and silver team medal,
    Pan American Games
Member, U. S. World Championship team

1988   Member, U. S. Olympic Fencing Team (Seoul)
        National Champion, men's sabre

1989   National Champion, men's sabre
        Member, U. S. World Championship team
        Eighth place, World Championships
        USFA Athlete of the Year

1990   Member, U. S. World Championship team

1991   Silver team medal, Pan American Games
        Member, U. S. World Championship team

1992   Member, U. S. Olympic Fencing Team
            (Barcelona)
        Flag bearer, closing ceremonies, Olympic Games

1995   Gold individual medal and silver team medal,
            Pan American Games
        Flag bearer, opening ceremonies, Pan American
            Games
        National Champion, men's sabre
        Sports Image Award

1996   Member, U. S. Olympic Fencing Team (Atlanta)
        F. Don Miller Award, USOC
        USFA Hall of Fame